POWER POSITION YOUR AGENCY

A Guide to Insurance Agency Success

The Troy Korsgaden Formula for
Insurance Management Professionals

Troy Korsgaden

Power Position Your Agency;
A Guide to Insurance Agency Success
The Troy Korsgaden Formula for Insurance Management Professionals

Editorial services for this book provided by
Laura Belgrave, editorial consultant for publishing professionals
Production by the Corsi Agency
Design & Graphics by Cecil Lopez

For information or for bulk purchase, please contact:

Troy Korsgaden Systems
Central Park Professional Center
1700 West Walnut Avenue, Suite A
Visalia, CA 93277

Phone: (800) 524-6390
Fax: (559) 625-4990
Email address:
troy@tkinsurance.com
Website: www.TKSystems.org

ISBN # 0-9701398-0-2

PRINTED IN THE UNITED STATES OF AMERICA

FOREWORD

Troy Korsgaden has a favorite expression. Whether he's in front of an audience or counseling one on one, he'll find the way to say, "Turn your wishes into committed goals."

Troy has transferred his agency goals to paper. He has mapped out his strategies for making good on his commitments. Troy has established an optimistic and meaningful philosophy in his agency. The ability to motivate is one of his most outstanding talents.

If there is any basis to the fact that we learn best from those who have already mastered the art, then ideas and information developed in *Power Position Your Agency; A Guide to Insurance Agency Success* can serve as a steppingstone to success for you.

The optimism Troy Korsgaden exudes and brings to everything he does permeates this book. You'll discover his proven strategies to be transferable and result producing.

Good Reading and Successful Selling!

Jack Kinder Jr. – Garry D. Kinder
Well-known Authors and Consultants

TABLE OF CONTENTS

INTRODUCTION

Greetings, welcome, and congratulations. You're obviously in the market for success and I can tell you right now that it's doable. Whether your agency is in a slumber mode and you want to wake it up or whether you're just contemplating launching your own agency, success is within reach.

You don't have to get there by throwing caution to the wind. You don't even have to take a big risk. What you do have to do is cast aside your fears and grab hold of the strategies in this book. They're simple. They're manageable. They work—and I should know. They've taken me from too few clients and too many sleepless nights to a more than comfortable living where I still have time to take my kids to Disneyland.

Bottom line? Life is good. But, of course, that's not how it started out . . .

I launched my agency in 1983. By the end of 1992, I had about 1,500 Policies in Force (PIF) to show for nine years' work. Even though I was working as hard or harder than ever before, I was struggling just to keep the status quo. Out of sheer frustration, I started developing systems that would make my agency and my time more productive. My systems weren't bad. In fact, they were good. But somehow, they proved to be problematic when I actually implemented them. Truthfully, I thought of bagging the whole lot of them more than once. Instead, I began to noodle around with refinements, and two things started to happen.

First, we began to grow. In just four years, we went from 1,500 PIF to more than 5,000 PIF. Now, we're at more than 6,350 PIF and as far as I'm concerned, we're still just getting started. Second, the fun of owning and operating my agency returned—and then some.

People started inviting me to speak at seminars across the United States. Before long, I learned what it was like to wake up in one city and go to sleep in another—and I enjoyed it! I still do. Sharing my ideas with thousands of agents was satisfying on a level I never anticipated in the days when I was just starting out. But it wasn't long before I realized that I couldn't always make a lasting effect during a two-hour presentation. After every seminar, our office would get bombarded by calls and visits from agents in search of a step-by-step procedure for implementing my systems in their agencies.

To answer all their requests and still achieve my own agency goal,

I needed to come up with something people could take away with them, something they could refer to again and again. That's when I decided to package my systems in an easy-to-understand book. It's what you're holding now. Don't look for voodoo fixes here. You won't find them. And don't look for "feel-good" advice that's more air than substance. You already know that won't work in our dynamic industry!

What you can expect to find in these pages is my formula for success in down-to-earth, specific steps. In Part I, I'll show you how to lay the foundation for rapid and sustained growth. In Part II, I'll detail the strategies you can use to support and extend your success.

And by the way, the size of your agency isn't a factor. Large and small agencies alike can benefit from using the systems in this book. In fact, the only thing you have to do to make the systems work on any level is commit to take action and make changes. I did it, and believe me, I'm no rocket scientist. You can, too.

So go for it! May you achieve the success you pursue!

Troy Korsgaden

PART ONE

Position Yourself
For Success

BUILD YOUR TOMORROWS
ON TODAY'S GOALS

A gents ask me all the time: "How do you consistently sell each line of insurance?" Well, the truth is there's no magic to what I do. In fact, my success springs from a premise that's so basic it almost sounds like a cliche: I have a *goal* for each line of insurance, and I make darn sure that I meet that goal. Plain and simple.

But I'd be lying if I said that's how I always operated. When I was starting out–and for longer than I care to admit–I thought it was enough to pump the phones for clients, shuffle paperwork from one pile to another, and keep a smile on my face when I went home at the end of a long day. You can be sure it kept me busy–and exhausted.

Besides, it wasn't like I didn't have ideas. I did, and lots of them, and most of them certainly did look like goals to me. But they weren't, not until I systematically put them on paper in a way that made them manageable. Then they became goals that I could reach. And once they became goals that I could reach, I began to realize success, the kind that almost feeds on itself.

I didn't have to get a degree in marketing, and in fact, I don't have one. All I did have to do was start with simple goals, keep them simple, and always, always hold them foremost in my strategies. And by the way, simple is key. For instance, if I want to achieve twenty life sales in a month, I don't set a goal for twenty sales a month, which can sound like a pretty tall order. Instead, I set it for "one a working day." Suddenly, the impossible seems possible. It sounds downright doable–and it is.

Motivate with Goals

It's easy to confuse fear with motivation. I did. In my early days it was fear that got me going. I raced around like someone was chasing me, always fearful that I wouldn't make my quota, that nobody would buy anything from me, that I'd fail altogether and finally just starve to death. What a lousy way to feel!

Well, maybe fear has its place, but besides taking the fun out of living it can also take the sleep out of sleeping. When that happens you know you're on the way to burnout. Anyone can do a sprint, but a marathon is another story and the reality is that no one can perform effectively for a prolonged period of time under the kind of stress that fear induces.

Clearly, I had to shake it off, and eventually I did. I traded it in for the kind of motivation that comes from well-planned goals; objectives that I wanted to reach. And this is important. When you set goals, make sure they're not goals placed on you by your manager or your company, but goals well planned by the only person who knows what you want most out of life—you!

I like two quotes that illustrate the need for setting your own goals and planning:

> *"Don't let other people tell*
> *you what you want."*
> --- Pat Riley,
> Basketball coach and author

> *"Don't let other people*
> *plan your future,*
> *because they don't have*
> *a lot planned for you."*
> --- Jim Rohn,
> Business philosopher

Of course, there's one more key to using goals as motivation: You have to be committed to doing the work required to achieve your goals. It's not as hard as you think.

Write It Down and Map It Out

A goal that isn't written down is only a wish, and you can't take wishes to the bank. It doesn't matter whether you've got your mind set on doubling your income or on achieving company awards, if you haven't written those objectives down as goals and mapped out a plan to reach them, what you want is almost sure to remain elusive. (Think not? Just consider how well you do when you go to the grocery store without a list—and that's way down the scale on easy goals!) The point is goals in your head and goals on paper are two different things, and you have to treat them that way.

Incidentally, I'm not suggesting that you can't start with goals in your head. There is something to be said for incubating ideas and concepts, for mulling things over. Just make sure you don't keep them there indefinitely. Break a couple of pencil leads and get them committed to paper. Then turn your goals into plans for action.

What you'll find along the way is that most goals are absolutely obtainable if you have enough reasons to obtain them. And the process itself is both painless and flexible, especially if you break your goals into incremental steps. When you do that, you can achieve what you want, not just for today but for as many tomorrows as you can get.

Here's how I go about it:

I begin the process of setting goals by backing into them. I don't look first at what tomorrow or the next week should bring, but where I want to be five years from now. In other words, my starting point begins five years in the future.

Then, once I'm satisfied that I genuinely know what I want from my business, I define goals that will help take me there, and I review them every year. But remember, those five-year goals constitute a starting point and to make sure they don't become overwhelming I reach for them through more modest measures. I break them into one-year goals. Goals that are one year off seem not only reasonable, but well within reach.

But even then, I don't stop. I break the one-year goals down further. I turn them into more specific monthly and weekly targets, and those become the workhorses of concrete achievement. When I look at something a month or a week away, I don't wonder if I can make it. I know I can. Best yet, I know that for every weekly or monthly goal I reach, I'm staying right on course toward my long-range goals.

I think of what I'm doing as creating maps. By now, the maps I create to achieve my goals are so specific that they've become my market-ing plans. The marketing plans define service, sales, and performance lev-els for each of my agency's departments. They're my blueprint for success.

To see what I'm talking about, check out **Appendix A**. Notice how I lay out my larger, more distant goals, and then break them into categories that I can comfortably handle in smaller increments. While you're looking it over, keep in mind what I said earlier about making things simple. I think you'll agree that my goal setting really can't get much more simple, and the beauty is that my strategy is effective! I always know where I'm going, and I have a clear path to get there.

Right about now, you may be saying, "Well sure, Troy, that's swell, but what about all the day-to-day stuff that comes up and kicks a hole in your planning? What do you do about the kinds of unexpected things that can steer you off course?"

It's a good question, and to some degree the answer is irrevocably linked with managing time, a subject I'll get to in Part II. Meanwhile, staying on top of goals–short and long term–calls for its own strategy, one that's designed specifically to stay a steady course on a daily basis.

The most effective method I've found to date that allows me to focus on top priority short-term goals is what I call the "Five Focus Goals" approach. Here's how it works:

Several times a day, I evaluate my performance in relation to my goals and plans, and I identify goals that require my specific time and attention over the next week. I list these goals on paper and keep them with me. Just as importantly, I go over them daily. As soon as one of the goals is accomplished, I take it off my list and replace it, so I always have five goals I'm working on.

Sometimes I make a list of the goals and share them with my staff. Other times, they're primarily for my personal attention. In any case, the Five Focus Goals method directs my attention and efforts to the priorities that I set.

In **Appendix B** you'll find a simple worksheet that you can use as is or adapt for your own means. Take a look at it, then check out the following example, which shows you how I fleshed out one of my own days on the form:

Goal #1	**Increase Life Count**
Action Plan:	A. Remind all employees to ask everyone they talk to!
	B. Send e-mail notes to remind all staff to call and ask.
	C. Day off contest for 4 applications in one day.

Goal #2	**Ask for Referrals**
Action Plan:	A. Remind clients of referral program.
	B. E-mail staff every day to ask.
	C. Update progress by tracking.

Goal #3	**Reduce Paperwork**
Action Plan:	A. Ask staff for input.
	B. Throw out anything you are not working on.

Goal #4	**Account Selling (Target market Household Program)**
Action Plan:	A. Review each household for selling strategy.
	B. Reward staff for add-on line of insurance.
	C. X-date sheet turned in every appointment.

Goal #5	**Sales Tract for Reviews and New Business**
Action Plan:	A. Finish draft.
	B. Have staff make changes.
	C. Send to graphic design.

Pretty simple, no?

Of course, you don't want to work in the dark. As your goals and plans become more specific, it's essential that they direct and motivate the efforts of all the employees in your agency. For that to happen, your goals need to become department- and employee-specific, and part of your management performance system. You'll read more about this shortly.

It bears repeating that setting and maintaining goals can and should be a simple process based on where you want to be, not where someone else thinks you should be. As you progress, you may find that your goals have progressed, too. Fine! Your goals should become bigger each year. Don't let them get too lofty, but make yourself stretch.

Involve Your Family

There's one last point to be made about goals, and it's important: Involve your family in the process. Part of the reason I'm so committed to my goals is that I know they help me provide what my family wants and needs. It's a great motivation. We share future aspirations and we understand what it's going to take from all of us to reach those goals. We try to keep a balance between work and home as we set goals so that when we ask, "Is the effort and sacrifice worth it?" we can answer, "Yes!"

Sure, there are bumps along the way. For me, probably the hardest part is to keep everything in balance. But when I do, it becomes a lot easier for all of us to accept that I sometimes need to leave early in the morning, come home at seven o'clock at night, or go out of town again.

For me, balance often involves short-term rewards for the family. I call them payoffs. For instance, my children love Disneyland, so we go to

Disneyland pretty often. Most often, that happens after I've been working especially hard. It's a payoff for them, and it's a payoff for me, and really, no matter how you slice it and dice it, the payoff comes from working toward a common goal.

Try it. You'll find that if your family is involved in mapping out goals right along with you, they'll be much more supportive and tolerant on those occasions when work cuts into your time with them. (Just make darn sure you come through with their payoff!)

You know, I can honestly say that after fourteen years, I still enjoy going to work. When I come home, I leave all the work at work, something not everybody can say. But it's easy for me to do that, because I accomplish the things I need to do during the day and then I separate my business and my personal life. It all comes together and gives me what I need. None of that would be possible without goals, and if that's a cliche, well, I can live with it. It works.

....

Troy's Bottom Line: Turn wishes into goals that will bring you to where you want to be by anchoring them to paper, then map out plans to reach your goals in manageable bites.

....

THE MAGIC BULLET: AN AGENCY CONTACT REPRESENTATIVE™

Wouldn't life be sweet if all the customers you could ever want simply walked through your door, begged you to sell them a policy and signed on the dotted line within a half-hour? You'd be done forever with chasing after clients, banging on doors and wondering where your next meal was coming from.

Well, what if I told you that not all of that is a pipe dream? What if I told you that you can prompt clients to come to you and that you actually can hit the point where you have to turn them away?

I'm not proposing that you do away with your car. What I am proposing is that you get yourself a magic bullet. I have one, otherwise known as an Agency Contact Representative", and if you do nothing else that I suggest in this book, do go out and get one for yourself. That person can turn your business around by freeing you up to do what you do best—sell insurance!

The Agency Contact Representative" does that by making the hardest sell of all—getting people to meet with you by scheduling eight to ten appointments a day. You read that right: eight to ten appointments a day, in your office, for twenty to thirty minutes each. And the beauty of it is this: The Agency Contact Representative's position can be wonderfully effective as a part-time job!

Let's face it, the days when you could sit back and wait for people to stroll into your office to buy insurance are long gone. To have a successful agency today, it's absolutely crucial that you be on the offense by proactively making contacts and setting appointments. There's no way around this. You have to find a way to have appointments with qualified people every day in order to talk to them about the products and services your agency offers.

Don't fool yourself by thinking you can do it alone. If you're wearing all the hats required to run an agency—salesperson, secretary, accountant, human resources manager and marketer—it's virtually impossible to focus on the most critical task of making contacts and getting the information you need for effective and timely sales presentations. That's where the Agency Contact Representative comes in. That's where the magic bullet finds its mark. I wish I had known it sooner.

Running in Circles

I knew a long time ago that the secret to success in this business is being in front of people. What I didn't know was how to do that and still take care of paperwork, phone calls, meetings, and everything else. There simply weren't enough hours in a day, and no matter how hard I worked, it seemed I never got ahead. I couldn't get in front of enough people to make my agency take off. Everything else was in the way.

Then, one day while I was brooding about business in the dentist's office, I noticed that the dentist had one employee, separate from everyone else, who stood out. All she seemed to be doing was pumping the phone, and either making appointments or rescheduling appointments. She didn't work on anyone's mouth. She didn't deal with accounting. The only thing she did was make sure that the dentist had someone in his chair.

Call it an epiphany if you want. All I know is that I was suddenly struck by what a simple but powerful business strategy this was, because if the dentist didn't have someone in his chair, he wouldn't have anything to bill out. The only things he would have were payments on his equipment and an unending stream of overhead costs. The person calling his clients was making sure that didn't happen. If it worked for him, I couldn't imagine why it couldn't work for me.

It could, and it did. Let me show you how.

Create The Agency Contact Representative's Role

First of all, banish the notion that you can't afford an Agency

Contact Representative (ACR). The truth is, you can't afford not to

have one.

Second, understand that in creating a position for an Agency

Contact Representative, you're creating a job for someone whose sole role

is to make sure you're in front of the right people to sell your product. The

ACR is not the person you want to stick with a thousand little jobs, the

kinds of things that crop up in any business. One hundred percent of the

ACR's time has to be directed toward calling current and prospective

clients to schedule, confirm, and reschedule appointments, and preparing

appointment folders after appointments are set. The ACR and agent work

together to set appointment goals, but it's the Agency Contact

Representative who carries them out.

By the way, goals for the appointments your ACR aims to sched-

ule should reflect whatever overall goals you're trying to achieve with your agency. For instance, in all the calls that my Agency Contact Representative makes in any given day, her goal is to get four appointments for policy review, two appointments for life insurance, two appointments for P&C (P&C for us means auto and home), and finally, two appointments a day for commercial insurance. Your goals will likely differ, but if you do this right you'll find that like me, you can indeed get ten appointments a day with people who value and take advice from a professional agent. And they'll be coming to see you. You won't be going to see them, which is the beauty of the ACR program.

The Position and Work

You'll love this: To do the job well, your ACR doesn't have to spend forty hours a week at it. Frankly, there's no reason in the world that the ACR position can't be a part-time job of about twenty hours per week, especially if you structure those hours for the most impact.

In this case, hours truly are a matter of quality, not quantity, and I've learned that the quality calling times are Monday through Thursday, from 2 p.m. to 7 p.m. That's not arbitrary. Believe me, I've tried combinations of hours any number of ways, and by now I'm past the point where I want to reinvent the wheel on it! But to break it down even further, the most ideal hours are from 2 p.m. to 5 p.m. when people can be contacted at work. Their day is winding down, and they would rather take the call there than at home when they're trying to put dinner on the table. The hours from 5 p.m. to 7 p.m. are reserved for reaching the small percentage of people who can't take a call at work or whose work number isn't available to you.

As far as Fridays go, I learned a long time ago not to bother with them. By Friday, most folks have the weekend on their minds and their interest in insurance drops in proportion to whatever fun things they're planning. Who can blame them?

If you use those time frames as a basic starting point, I think you'll quickly see that a good ACR can make approximately forty calls an hour using introduction lists, which I'll discuss in Part II. Clearly, that doesn't mean your ACR will connect with forty people. He or she is bound to hit busy signals, wrong numbers and no answers. But dialing forty numbers absolutely does make it possible for the ACR to get enough valid responses for you to meet your objective: eight to ten people in front of you every day.

Of course, your ACR needs to begin with qualified leads that you provide. But what you'll find is that as your ACR grows in the position, he or she will become instrumental in acquiring and developing effective introduction lists that will continually fuel your agency–and keep your appointment book filled.

Scripts

After a while, don't be surprised if you think your Agency Contact Representative walks on water. Just don't expect that the first day. Especially in the beginning, you can't expect an Agency Contact Representative to simply pick up the phone and know exactly what to say in order to book appointments. You also can't expect your ACR to know how best to deal with tricky situations or reluctant clients.

That's where scripts come in. A good script helps the Agency Contact Representative control the conversation and guide people to set an appointment. In a perfect world, they wouldn't be needed. But your ACR will undoubtedly encounter plenty of objections to setting appointments such as, "I'm too busy to schedule with you," or "Is this really important?" Another favorite objection that you're all familiar with–the kind that can make you wince—is, "Can't I just get a quote over the phone?"

Clearly, your ACR must be shotgun ready to override those and other objections, and a script can help. You'll find examples of good scripts in Appendix C. Use them as a starting point and then create some of your own to fit your unique philosophy and personality. Put together a different script for each line of insurance you're marketing, and make sure scripts are always in front of your ACR during calls.

From the Phone to the Calendar

Calls are one thing. Getting appointments on the book is another. Whatever you do, don't make the mistake of hogging your calendar or scribbling down outside appointments on scraps of paper that float around on your desk. You know how it goes with good intentions. You might think you'll get around to incorporating those notes into the office calendar later, but if you get distracted you'll be crippling yourself. You'll also be crippling your Agency Contact Representative, because your ACR must have immediate access to an updated calendar to be effective.

For that matter, not just any old calendar will do. Given the dynamic nature of our business, a computerized calendar is critical. So if you're still a little gun shy about using them, get over it fast. The simple truth is that a rigid appointment calendar will limit your ACR's ability to schedule appointments, while a flexible schedule will result in more appointments. More appointments mean you're in front of more people. Being in front of more people is what will bring you the greatest success.

Appointment Files

Your Agency Contact Representative's greatest gift will be what he or she can do on the phone. Unquestionably, calling is what will take most of the ACR's day. But there's another part of your ACR's job that you won't want to let slide, and it has to do with files.

All appointments that get set for you need to be married to a file before you ever set eyes on the client. That file should be created by your Agency Contact Representative and should include:

• A printout of appointment in the computer or on the calendar
• Pre-appointment information forms
• A printout of the information on the office database for current clients
• Any information that may assist a sale (just married, new baby, etc.)

You may want more information, but don't settle for less. You'll want to be reminded of details concerning existing clients. You'll want to know whatever you can about new clients coming in the door. Let your Agency Contact Representative help. After all, it's the ACR who will present the first welcoming voice on the phone.

Find the Right Person

You already know how important good scripts can be in helping your Agency Contact Representative blaze through forty phone calls every hour. Understand, however, that no matter how terrific those scripts are, they're nothing if your ACR doesn't have good delivery and–as importantly–a fundamental conviction in what you're trying to accomplish.

So what makes for an Agency Contact Representative with all the right qualities? Minimally, you need someone who's upbeat, talkative, friendly, and projects a good attitude. Beyond that, you're after someone self-sufficient and resourceful. Put those qualities together and you'll find that you're really looking for candidates who don't accept "no" too easily, but also don't come across as pushy.

Of course, you'll want your Agency Contact Representative to be someone who embraces your agency's philosophy of insurance, and genuinely believes that people have a need for the products and services you offer. But that doesn't mean you have to limit your search to a pool of candidates with insurance backgrounds. ACRs don't need to be trained in specific insurance products or have prior insurance knowledge. They do need to know—and be persuasive in conveying—why clients should come into your office to meet with you.

This may surprise you, but I've found that it's generally most effective to hire an ACR from outside your agency as opposed to someone who already works on your team. Coming in "from the cold" helps a new Agency Contact Representative stay focused on his or her goals, and if for no other reason than the person won't understand how to help your other staff members, which means far fewer distractions. After all, getting sidetracked is the last thing you want for the person who's trolling for appointments on your behalf.

Believe it or not, finding the right person to be your Agency Contact Representative isn't hard. I keep my eyes open everywhere I go for people who could potentially fit into a position in my agency, and particularly to identify people who might have the characteristics I'm looking for in an ACR.

I've found that good ACRs are more highly qualified than an average $6-an-hour telemarketer–and they should be paid more, too. It is full time pay for part time work. Some of the people I've found to be successful Agency Contact Representatives include frontline workers in the service industry, drama students, portrait studio workers, and telemarketers who contact me with impressive sales pitches.

If you're wondering what kind of classified ad can draw qualified applicants for an Agency Contact Representative position, take a look at the following samples. Both have worked for me.

CUSTOMER SERVICE TRAINEE
We need a mature, reliable, helpful, friendly, professional, positive person to help us with our busy insurance office. We will provide all training and a professional workplace. Work hours for this position are: Mon-Thurs, 2 p.m. to 7 p.m. Permanent position with growth potential. $10/hour. Call 555-4689.

CUSTOMER SERVICE REP
Office help needed to recontact existing clients and schedule appointments for Insurance Agency in Visalia. Mon-Thurs, 2 p.m. to 7 p.m. $10/hour. Call 555-5773.

Having an Agency Contact Representative is like having a goose that lays golden eggs. The Agency Contact Representative is the goose, and the appointments are the golden eggs. The proven "Law of Large

Numbers" attests that if you talk to enough people, a certain number of them will buy from you. Getting those people to talk to you to begin with starts with the Agency Contact Representative. Find the right person and you can count on a steady stream of sales opportunities and income.

....

Troy's Bottom Line: Agency Contact Representatives are the lifeblood of growth. You're not doomed without one, but you'll flourish if you get one.

....

REPLACE YOURSELF—AND WATCH YOUR AGENCY GROW!

L et's assume you're good at what you do. No. Scratch that. Let's assume you're very good at what you do, maybe even extraordinary. But if being exceptional hasn't exactly translated into hard dollars and cents yet, it may be because you haven't replaced yourself—and you should.

I'm only half kidding. The awful truth is that an agency stuck in the mud is often stuck there because the boss—you—can't let go. I know. I was one of those bosses. I was the guy who did everything. The problem with that strategy (if you can even call it a strategy) is that you're spread too thin.

Quite simply, if you're trying to do a thousand different things, none of them gets done right. Where that particularly stings is in sales, the one thing you probably do better than anything else, and the only thing that can get your agency out of first gear. I know this probably sounds like a broken record by now, but remember that the name of the game is being in front of people. You can't do that if you're shuffling papers and answering the phone every time it rings.

When I decided to change the way I ran my business, I adopted this important principle: If you have a job to do and you can hire someone to do it, make the hire! That principle has worked so well that if you were to say to me, "Troy, what's the main reason for your agency's growth?" I could only respond, "I'm surrounded by people with great attitudes who work well together."

Believe me, I didn't start out with eleven employees. In fact, I started out like many of you, with none. But hiring an Agency Contact Representative was a wake-up call. She put so many prospective clients in front of me that the results were staggering. Really, she was making me make money, serious money, and it was a heady feeling! Somehow, though, I managed not to dash out and buy a Mercedes Benz, a tendency many agents have. Instead, I invested the money back into my agency. I sat down and decided what I wanted my agency to look like. Then, I hired employees to replace myself, and worked with them to create a high performance work team.

My Own Agency, Then and Now

Of course, you can't go out and hire a fully developed agency staff when you're only at 1,500 policies in force. But after reading *The E myth* by Michael Gerber, I realized it's important to have an idea of what you want your agency to look like down the road. To show you how those structures can change, first take a look at the organizational chart for my agency in 1990:

Exhibit C

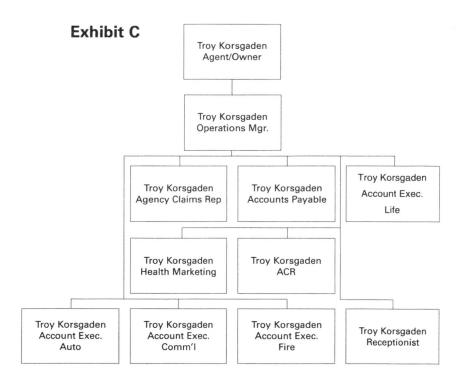

Wow. That Troy Korsgaden . . . look at his name in all those boxes. He sure was a worker bee! True enough. I was definitely working, and working hard. But for growth, the objective is to replace your name in each box by delegating the work to an employee. That's what I did and if you look at the organizational chart showing my agency at 5,200 policies in force, I think you'll see just how thoroughly I managed to replace myself.

Exhibit D

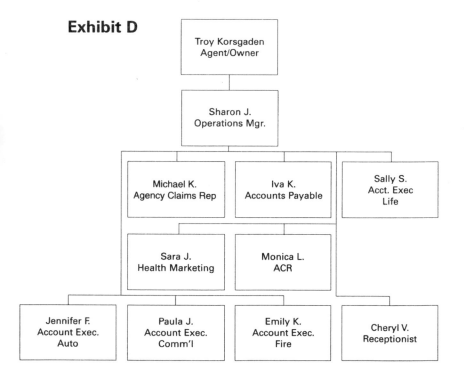

I bet I don't have to tell you how nice it was not to have to do it all!

Naturally, though, growth doesn't happen overnight. You have to set priorities and always, always keep in mind the goals you originally established.

Here are the basic tenets to grow your agency, which most assuredly can guide you out of every job that distracts you from being in front of people and making sales:

Hire an Agency Contact Representative first—even before the receptionist! I'll say it again: An Agency Contact Representative is the magic bullet that propels growth. (You'll find a specific job description for the Agency Contact Representative position and others in **Appendix D.**)

Once you've taken on an Agency Contact Representative and you're seeing the results—which you will—go after some other people to replace yourself with. Define a manageable scope and create a specific job description for each new position. Make sales, insurance review and overall agency management the very last roles to delegate. (And by the way, this doesn't have to happen all at once; it's taken me more than five years to get everything in place to begin delegating parts of these roles.)

Think through every role you create, and in every case where you're bring-ing someone new aboard, make sure you don't expect that person to be good at a hundred different things. It's tempting to do that, but if wearing too many hats wasn't effective for you, it won't be for your staff people, either.

Specify the one or two goals you expect to reach by hiring each new employee. This doesn't mean that there shouldn't be cross training and some sharing of job functions, but it's important that each employee under-stand exactly what he or she is responsible for, and how you will measure performance.

In my agency, the first job I wanted to delegate was handling monthly pay problems. If your experience is anything like mine, you know why. The monthly bill tends to be one area that gets messed up more often than others, and it has the most questions and delinquent payments. I wanted it off my back so I could focus on goals that would help me grow. Well, because the biggest area in my agency with monthly pay is auto, I decided to find someone who would take care of auto policies.

I knew I wanted someone personable, and before long I found a customer service representative (CSR). I didn't make the job more complicated than it needed to be. In fact, I intentionally kept the scope of the position narrow and, in turn, I expected my CSR to be very good at processing auto applications. As time progressed, my first CSR actually did become an auto expert by asking questions and finding answers on her own. And while she developed knowledge of fire and life insurance lines, she continued to focus on auto—and do a great job!

As the business grew, I hired other CSRs to become experts in my other insurance lines—in fire, then life, and finally, commercial. Having them has made an enormous difference for me and it can for you too.

Go for Attitude, Not Experience

Let me tell you a story about one of my employees. She had worked at my bank for a couple of years. The bank was across the street, and I would go in every day, always in a hurry. It seemed that whenever I was in the bank, I'd hear her saying something like, "Oh, Mr. Jones, let me open up" if all the other windows were busy, or, "Mr. Anderson, I know you're busy. Let me take care of this for you and I'll just go ahead and mail your receipt."

I got the same royal treatment. When I came into the bank, she would say, "Hey Troy, I know you're busy, let me do this paperwork. We'll run it across the street for you."

I loved it. I loved the thoughtfulness. I loved how sincerely she seemed to put her customers' needs first. Before long, I thought to myself, "This is the kind of person I want working for me." Who wouldn't?

Well, the next time I had a position in my agency, I walked across the street, gave my card to her, and said, "Whenever you want to work in a place where you can make more money and have more fun, will you please give me a call? We've got a spot just for you. We're always looking for people with your kind of attitude."

She was in my office looking for a job the next day.

The point of the story is that in hiring people, attitude is everything. Honestly, it's far more important than any office skills a person may have. You can always train people for the specifics of a job, but you can't teach them how to have a good attitude. They either have it or they don't. I want the ones who do.

Attitude is so important to me that before I hire people, I tell them, "We have a good attitude in the office. If you wake up in a bad mood, when you come to the office, fake it. Sooner or later you'll feel better." That's not just bunk. Think about how many times you've been in situations where one person's lousy attitude spilled over onto everybody else. Well, the same can work in reverse. A good attitude fuels other good attitudes. In fact, corny as it may sound, I like the adage, "Attitudes are contagious: Is yours worth catching?"

Beyond attitude, you really don't need to look for people who already come with insurance experience. All you need are people who are willing to learn. Look, the simple truth is that the insurance business isn't all that complicated. If you have a specific job description and performance standards, you can teach new hires the nitty gritty of the job you need them to do.

There's another plus in hiring people who don't necessarily have insurance backgrounds: They won't have to unlearn any bad habits. Actually, my own preference in hiring is to find people who specifically don't already have experience. People with previous exposure to the insurance business probably learned it from another agent, and that agent may not share my philosophies or do business the way I do. So I like to start from scratch, build a foundation of trust and mutual respect with new employees, and see that they learn my business my way. That approach hasn't hurt me. Time and again, I've been impressed with the results new hires can achieve even if they're new to office work.

It's exhilarating to watch your agency grow, and you'll want to make sure you keep it moving at a comfortable pace by being prepared to hire quickly when you're ready to fill a new position or when someone leaves. If you move too slowly, not only will things inevitably back up on you, but also when you eventually do fill your slot, the new person will be starting at a disadvantage. Clearly, that's the last thing you need when you're all trying to get off to a good start.

But finding someone to fill positions quickly and effectively doesn't have to mean thumbing through a phone book for decent employment agencies. All you have to do is look for the right person before you even know you need one. That's not as nuts as it sounds. Here's how I go about it:

First, every time I meet someone with a good personality who I'd want to work with, I jot down his or her name, along with the person's strengths and weaknesses. Whenever I need a new employee, I review the information I've collected and work from it to begin developing a list of solid candidates.

Second, because I know my current employees have good atti-tudes–they wouldn't be working for me if they didn't–I can safely speculate that they associate with other people who have good attitudes. So if some-thing is opening up in my agency, I ask around the office for suggestions on candidates. Water does seek its own level and I'd be foolish to overlook the resources that can come from my own staff.

But no matter how potential candidates come to mind we track them in an "Employee Prospect Book" maintained in the office. The book contains the information on a form like this:

Employee Prospect

Name_____

Address_____

City/State/Zip_____

Home Phone _____

Work Phone _____

Cell Phone_____

Current Employer_____

Current Position/Title _____

Where would this person fit in our office?

_____

_____

_____

There's nothing fancy about the form, but fancy has never been our style. Results are, and looking ahead produces them.

....

Troy's Bottom Line: Wearing too many hats will only wear you down. Surround yourself with good people and let them wear the hats instead. You'll be free to focus on what you do best–selling insurance.

....

CREATE A HIGH PERFORMANCE TEAM

I f you're going to bother to replace yourself with dynamic, enthusiastic people, the last thing in the world you want is to make them go solo. All that'll happen is you'll wind up sacrificing the energy and good ideas they can collectively create if you do.

In our office, that's one reason we're adamant about approaching work by using a team concept. A good team has the ability to recognize problems and opportunities fast, and then carry out good decisions. But if you really want your agency to move off the charts, then go all out and build something that exceeds an "out the door at five o'clock mentality." Go for the ultimate–a high performance team.

I'm lucky. I have one, and it was built on a foundation of trust and with a good attitude that stays flexible, open, and growing. With my high performance team, there are clear, properly developed goals, objectives, and expectations. We all focus on our strengths, because those are the only tools each of us has. We're all ready to take on new and different challenges, problems and opportunities.

In a very real sense, the people in my office are my family away from home. I care about them, and we really relate to each other. And actually, it goes beyond that: We're accountable to each other. We all know that each person is significant and unique, and important to the success of the operation. We try to interact in the kind of positive way that creates synergy, which compounds our resources for positive results. We're fair with each other and respect integrity.

That's not just a lot of "feel good" mumbo-jumbo. It's real, and it's there because we all insist on open communication, which creates shared meaning and shared understanding. If you think the qualities I've described are just plain silly, or even unnecessary, just poke your head into most offices today. How many people look happy to be there?

Make no mistake. Teamwork, with a high performance team, is crucial to achieving your goals. But it's not something you can pluck off a shelf at the corner store. You have to create team spirit and you have to work at keeping it. No, it's not always easy. How many of the good things in life are? It is important, though. In fact, if you're not proud of each member of your staff—if you don't think they're the best—then you need to make some changes now!

Begin at the Beginning–with Conviction

You're in the business you're in because you believe in it. You're convinced that what you do helps people. But for your office staff to come together as a high performance team, they have to believe it, too. They have to be convinced that what they do and how they do it makes a positive and significant difference in the lives of the clients the agency serves.

That's the founding principle for a high performance team, and it begins with a common understanding of and commitment to the agency's philosophy. Obviously, you can tell your staff members what you believe in and why. And you should! But in the same way that wishes grow into goals when you write them down, your own philosophy becomes more concrete when you put it on paper. Specifically, your philosophy on paper is a commitment. It's your mission statement.

You don't need to drone on endlessly in a mission statement. They're not legal documents or marketing plans. They're your personal and business statements of philosophy and include an overview of the principles that guide your thinking. If you don't already have one, please do yourself the favor of creating one. (See an example of the mission statement governing my own agency's philosophy in **Appendix A**.)

Of course, there are also concrete ways you can help your employees absorb and believe in what your agency stands for. Let them observe a claim settlement. Encourage them to talk with other agents about good and bad claims experiences. Ask them if they've ever talked to the family member of someone who died with no insurance; ask what impact that had. Even encourage your staff members to take a field trip to a mortuary to learn about the costs involved in death and burial, and the circumstances of families who must take out loans to finance those expenses.

You can undoubtedly think of other strategies that will encourage your employees to become active participants in your business, rather than just observers on the periphery. And that's a good thing! Involvement can only underscore the importance of what you do and why you do it. Underscoring that importance leads to conviction. Conviction leads to a high performance team.

My employees are convinced that we have a great agency, that we give great service for a fair price, and that we add value to our clients' insurance programs. They also know that people can get cheaper insurance, but that they can't get any better agency to work for them.

When your staff members have this kind of conviction, they'll want to get clients into your office to talk about insurance. They'll understand that when clients come in, they'll get the best buy and know that their time was well spent.

I start creating that conviction the first day I meet a potential employee. I tell the candidate how great our office is, and how fortunate he or she would be to join our staff. And I back it up by demonstrating my agency's principles every day.

Performance Management

Here's a no-brainer: A high performance team is comprised of high performing individuals. But that's not automatic. Selective hiring is a good start, but even the best hires require support from clear goals and performance expectations, consistent employee development, effective discipline, and fair and motivating compensation to optimize their performance.

Take a look at the components that will keep your high performance team operating at mach speed:

You have a choice to make. Beginning with day one, you can help new employees succeed, or you can help them fail. Obviously, you'll want them to succeed, but don't imagine for a moment that their success is entirely up to them. Your role in how well they do is as big or bigger than theirs. And if you make it a priority to help them develop goals to work toward, they'll be light years ahead of those who work in the dark elsewhere. Clearly defined goals help employees achieve your objectives for them.

Unless you're from another planet, the biggest overall goal you'll likely set for most staff members is for them to increase income. The insurance business isn't a chapter from *Rebecca of Sunnybrook Farm*. Like most industries, it's a dynamic business propelled by money. No money, no forward movement—plain and simple. Whether employees know anything about insurance or not, they need to know that.

Look, when I make new hires, I want them to understand that I've brought them aboard because I want them and their ability to increase income. And by the way, there's a distinct difference between want and need. You might need a receptionist because there are a hundred phone calls coming in and you've just got to have someone to answer the phone. But if someone is joining my auto, fire, or life departments, I don't need the person, I want the person. Those kinds of positions are basically expansion positions. I want the people who fill them because I want increased profit. And if I'm going to spend a dollar on their salary, I expect two to come back. They need to know this right up front, and they might need to be reminded from time to time.

I use a basic scenario to describe how capitalism works in our business. I explain that if we make $1 million this year, and $1.3 million next year, that means there's additional money to pay for raises, bonuses, a better office, additional staff, and more. On the other hand, if we only make $900,000 next year, there's less to pay for the things we want, and some things have to be cut. I take the time to explain how much better it is for all of us if there's more profit.

Now then, if you're rolling your eyes and thinking to yourself, "Troy, everyone knows that," well, you'd be right–and . . . not so right. True, the profit concept is pretty simple. But experience has absolutely taught me that it's a business basic that needs to be explained and reinforced.

For that matter, my basic explanation goes beyond a simple lesson on the value of profit. Once new staff members understand how profit can bode well not just for me, but for them, I take it a step further. I explain how they can impact profit directly, as individuals and as members of a dynamic team. In other words, I let them know that what they do on a daily basis affects the bottom line and I encourage them to expand their value by creating new systems to increase productivity and sales. Call it a lesson in capitalism if you want. It makes a difference in how committed your staff members remain in helping you achieve agency goals.

Naturally, you'll have other, more job-specific goals for every staff member as well. Just make sure that whatever you set out for them is attainable and that they genuinely believe that those goals are attainable. Don't just drop a job description and a list of goals on their desk and expect them to wing it. Show them how simple it can be to achieve goals. Reiterate that they're not on their own, that they can work together with you to reach their goals. And then remind them that if they reach their goals, more revenue will float into the agency. If there's more revenue, they're going to make more money.

By now, I'm sure you see that there's some maintenance involved here. You've got to talk to employees on a regular basis if you're going to motivate them and help them focus on doing the things that will bring success. It's easy to get snowed under with work—I bet your desk is overflowing, even as you read this—but if days without discussion slide into weeks, don't be surprised if your employees lose sight of their goals. And I'm no saint when it comes to this myself. I constantly remind myself to find out what it is an employee wants or needs to meet goals, and to figure out how to parlay those wants or needs into a win-win situation.

Here's a promise: If you work with the members of your high performance team to achieve common goals, not only will you get there—and reap the rewards with them—but you'll all have a lot more fun in the process! Guaranteed.

Evaluations and Development

Want to know how you're doing with your business? All you have to do is look at your balance sheet. But what about the people who work for you? Assuming they don't read tea leaves, how are they supposed to gauge how well they're doing?

Well, the expression on your face may tell them something, but it's not enough. Employees need concrete feedback and despite the many and varied business tools developed over the years, there still isn't anything that tops an employee review. The concept shouldn't make your staff members break out in a cold sweat. If you go about the review process systematical-ly, on schedule, and in a proactive fashion, both you and your employees will benefit.

In my office, I sit down with each employee to review his or her performance and set new goals after the first three months of employment. After that, I conduct reviews at least every year, and sometimes every six months. I approach evaluations with two objectives: to provide feedback for my staff members and to get feedback from them. In other words, reviews are a time to listen and learn for both of us. So what goes on dur-ing the review process?

First, we talk about the employee's productivity and achievement of the specific goals we set when the person was hired, or since his or her last evaluation. Next we review any customer satisfaction feedback. Then I encourage the employee to talk about how things are going and I solicit ideas on how we might improve office systems or generate more business. I ask about the employee's aspirations, and what specific duties and goals he or she might have for future performance. From there, we set future roles and performance goals.

Notice that I've put a lot of emphasis on "we." That's because the most effective kind of employee review should be an exchange that goes both ways. Time and again, I've found that a two-way review discussion provides terrific direction and motivation for employee development and for agency goals and problem solving.

It isn't enough, however, to walk away from a review session feeling warm and bubbly. Remember, reviews aren't just about how well any given employee is doing. They're forward-looking exercises that should include a strategy to help the employee grow even more. So in my office, the review isn't over until my staff member and I work to create specific opportunities for the further development of skills and job roles.

For example, as a customer service representative becomes an expert in her specific area and learns more about the range of insurance products that we offer, she has the opportunity to turn customer service into sales. As she demonstrates the ability to sell, I may support her with an Agency Contact Representative to fill her schedule. If she's been showing me what she can do, you bet I'm going to provide the resources for her to do it well! It's that win-win concept again, and it works. In fact, I go into the hiring process with the idea that anyone I bring aboard has to have potential to become an associate in the agency.

In a more general sense, I try to stay savvy about employee development on a continuing basis, not just at the time of a review. I try to create a culture and environment that supports self-improvement and learning. This isn't just some platitude. Our industry is ever changing and you know as well as I that we're all goners if we don't keep up. We have to make learning a daily process, for us and for our team members.

I do this by listening to tapes, taping myself, and reading books, and I encourage my staff members to do the same. If one of my employees tells me about a book or a tape set or anything that would improve him or her, I say, "Good. Here's the credit card. Go buy it and let's all learn from it." After all, who can argue with someone bent on enhancing performance? Besides, there's a side benefit from that single purchase. Ultimately, the book or tape prompts us to set aside time to share ideas and think about where and how we need to improve.

You can always take the concept even further. One of the things I sometimes do when an employee has performed particularly well is to encourage the person to spend a "weekend away" reading a self-improvement book or listening to some tapes. I pay for the person's hotel room at the beach, and the person gets a break and some time to invest in their own development.

Discipline

Here's the ugly truth: It's not a perfect world, and not all employees do what they're supposed to do when they're supposed to do it. That can be bad news not just for you, but for everybody else in your office who does perform well. It's also why discipline is an essential component of performance management.

The problem is, poor performers drag the whole team down. When I hire people, I tell them right up front, "Here are the boundaries. Stay inside of them and you'll be successful. Step outside of them, and you'll be gone." Maybe that sounds blunt or even harsh, but I've found that employees would much rather hear it up front than learn it on their way out. Here are some examples of what I mean about stepping outside the boundaries of expected performance:

- Coming to work late
- Dressing inappropriately at the office, where we maintain a professional standard of attire that includes ties for men and business clothing for women (which can include slacks)
- Missing work beyond what might be expected for sick days, or missing work in suspicious patterns
- Having a bad attitude
- Stealing
- Annoying other people in the office

Occasionally, I have people who don't work out, and I confess that sometimes I've blown the right way to resolve a bad situation. I hope you won't repeat the biggest mistake I've made in dealing with some of them: waiting and hoping that their performance would turn around. It hardly ever does, so act now to move "out of line" employees away from your organization—quickly!

Pay is Important

Don't fool yourself. No matter how terrific you are as a boss, no matter how effectively you work with your staff members, no matter how pleasant you've made your office environment, pay is important to your employees. You have a bottom line. So do they.

I pay more than the other agencies in my area. I aim to pay about twenty percent more. I do that because I've learned that to get the best people, I need to be as competitive with pay as I am with any other part of my business strategy. But before you set or alter your own pay structure, you need to know the going rate in your town. Once you've got that, aim higher. Your goal is to attract and keep motivated people who will work together as a high performance team. You need to make your objectives their own, and you need to make it worth their while.

Aside from paychecks, though, I've also found that performance rewards make for another great employee motivator. An example of pay incentives is the one I've structured for my customer service representatives. I have a "minimum new business quota" for my CSRs. But beyond that, when a CSR can work independently I pay a salary plus twenty percent of the "Agency New Business Commission" for additional sales. It's a powerful inducement for generating more income for the agency and money for the CSR. In fact, the extra money often amounts to an incentive of up to thirty percent of the base salary.

When I hire people, I tell them, "Do a good job and I'll pay you. If you do more than I expect, I'm going to pay you even more. Let's have fun!"

I just told you that if you compensate employees for achievement, they'll stretch in achievement and bring revenue into your agency. It's a time-honored strategy that has proven its mettle more than once, and for more than one industry.

Know this, however: It isn't the only strategy, it isn't always the most effective strategy, and it shouldn't be your only strategy. If you listen to your employees you'll learn what else matters to them as well. Sometimes, it's as simple as making accommodations in work schedules.

For instance, when my Agency Contact Representative originally came in to interview, it quickly became clear that money wasn't the issue. In fact, more important to her was flexibility. She told me that her husband was a teacher and when he had time off, she wanted to share that time with him and her family. I could hardly argue with the value in that. Of course, the biggest concern for me was whether she would be able to meet the goals and objectives that I had for her. I had to be convinced that she could get the job done effectively in a scenario that was different from what I originally had in mind. But I didn't automatically dismiss the notion out of hand. Instead, she talked, I listened. I talked, she listened. We hammered out an arrangement based on give and take, and negotiated a very satisfactory employment agreement that included time off work hours.

Another example of building flexibility into a work agreement was demonstrated with my auto CSR, a mother of two small children, whose family was very important to her. We worked out a flexible three-day workweek and because her performance remained consistently high she did the same amount of work as a full time person. The arrangement turned into a win-win for both her and the agency. The agency's auto department production increased, and my CSR got the time she wanted with her family.

Depending on your own circumstances, you might find other measures that can stretch better than a buck. Be creative! The idea is to listen to what your employees tell you is important, and then be receptive to meeting their needs. When you do, they'll respond in more ways than you can count.

Staff Meetings

Volumes have been written on how best to conduct staff meetings, and I'm not going to rehash what's been done so well by so many in the field. What I will say, however, is that holding staff meetings on a regular basis is vital. In my office, staff meetings help to reinforce the team aspect of the agency. They also keep me plugged in on levels where I might not otherwise keep the connection, and that connection is crucial. It's my agency and I darn well better stay aware of what's going on in it!

Sometimes staff meetings seem like a low priority, but I've found that on occasions when I start feeling like we're spinning out of control, we've simply gone too long without a staff meeting. And I'm sure you know what that out-of-control feeling is all about. To borrow a cliche, it's that old "one hand doesn't know what the other hand is doing." It may stem from a lack of communication, or from something else altogether. The symptom matters less than the cure, and the cure for me is a staff meeting, which I conduct at least twice a month.

Of course, I don't go into staff meetings on empty. To make them productive, I bring along a planned agenda. The agenda is based, in part, on the annual marketing plan and–you won't be surprised by now–my own "Five Focus Goals." One way or another, goals make up the big picture, and I never want my high performance team to stray far from it.

Morale

You've probably heard it said about any job that when it stops being fun, it's time to get out. The sentiment makes a lot of sense, especially when you really think about how much time people spend at their jobs. I'm not saying that work needs to be a slam-dunk in terms of entertainment, but should work be fun? Yes. In fact, I'll go out on a limb here: People need to have fun at work!

I'm talking about morale. I don't know about you, but a long face at work can drag me down. It can drag even the heartiest souls down, so I really make a conscious effort to keep morale up—not always an easy task. Let's face it, there are only so many hours in a day and it's all too easy to get busy and grow unaware of the office environment. But you just can't let that happen.

So how do you avoid poor morale? For one thing, watch for signals—like those long faces—and find out what's causing them. For another, keep your ears and eyes open to find people doing something right, and praise them for work well done. Finally, avoid creating an atmosphere in which your staff members cringe if they make a mistake –
Doers make mistakes!

We all make errors and, for that matter, if mistakes never happen, growth would probably take a nosedive. Look at the "doer's" of the world. If they seem to make more mistakes than anyone, it's because they're trying new things—and good for them! Creativity is what brings us all to the next level.

My own strategy in dealing with someone who makes a mistake is to simply not make a big deal out of it. I work with the person to fix the mistake and we go about our business. For some, maybe that's enough. But too often people feel miserable way out of proportion to the mistake they made, so I try to give them a pat on the back as soon as possible. I don't think that's going overboard. What I do think is that it encourages experimentation, creates loyalty and gives everyone a feeling of belonging to a team—a high performance team.

Isn't that what *you* want?

Troy's Bottom Line: Turn your staff into a high performance team by building a foundation of trust and conviction. You'll never have to wing it again–and you'll have more fun.

PART TWO

The Nitty-Gritty of Success

GET A GRIP ON TIME

There are only twenty-four hours in a day and no one is inventing any more. As business philosopher Jim Rohn says, "Rich people have twenty-four hours in a day and poor people have twenty-four hours in a day. You have twenty-four hours and I have twenty-four hours. You can't save time, you can only use it effectively."

Jim will never get an argument out of me on that! I doubt he'll get one from you, either. No matter how you slice'em and dice'em, it's what you do with the hours in a day that spells the difference between success and failure in achieving your goals.

The Right End of the Bull

Effective time management isn't something that came to me automatically. I had to horse around with the bull first, which isn't as strange as it sounds. See, when I first started I found that I was spending way too much time at home watching Gilligan's Island and Brady Bunch re-runs . . . that sort of thing. What I wasn't doing was having appointments.

Obviously, I was suffering a bad case of lousy time management.

I gave it some thought—not enough, as it turned out—and concluded that I'd better spend more time in the office if I wanted to grab the bull by the tail.

Funny thing about that tail, though. Once I grabbed onto it, all it did was drag me all over the place. You know what I'm talking about. The phone would ring and I'd snap it up. If someone needed an answer, I'd fumble all over the place until I could get it. In other words, I tackled whatever came to my attention the moment it came to my attention. Fast and efficient—that's what I thought I was being.

Well, I had the "fast" part right. But efficient? Uh-uh. I wound up being late for appointments, and then apologizing for being late. Every time I turned around, it seemed like I was apologizing for something. It had to stop. I began to re-evaluate my approach and in the process, I realized that I'd inadvertently put myself on the defense, when what I needed was to be on the offense. The only way I could get there was to get a grip on time.

Getting on the offense didn't happen overnight, but once I achieved that goal, the bull stopped dragging me around. In fact, I let go of the bull's tail altogether and grabbed it by the nose ring instead. Guess who's dragging whom now?

If you're anything like me, your gut probably tells you whether you're managing your time effectively. I have my own internal "uptight meter" and it shrieks at me if I'm not. For instance, if the day is a busy one but I've got a grip on time because I'm staying focused on my priorities, I manage to stay relatively calm inside. You can give me your best shot and I'm not going to get thrown off course. But if I feel more and more uptight when things start to go wrong, I know I need to sit down and figure out what I can do to manage my time better.

Sometimes, even seemingly small situations can set your uptight meter off. For me, stuff piling up on my desk used to do it. If the piles got too high—especially just before a trip out of town—the hairs on my arms would practically stand up in a salute to tension. The horror wasn't just that I sensed I was losing control. It was also embarrassment. I wanted to look organized, and stacks of papers fluttering everywhere was anything but!

Good time management is like stepping on the accelerator—the better you manage your time, the faster you can go, without sacrificing efficiency, without slamming into walls. In fact, good time management can enable you to achieve things that seem downright impossible. Here's an example of effective time management from my own life:

My daughter became ill with a rare virus that kept her in the hospital for sixty days. The hospital was an hour away by car and I visited her every day. It killed my agency, right? Wrong. I did more accounts in the first six months than I did all of the previous year!

Even though I spent two hours each day driving to the hospital and back, I still kept eight to twelve appointments a day. How did I do it? I planned. I just had to do my appointments at different times. Each day from 6 a.m. to 8 a.m. was packed with appointments, phone calls, and whatever else needed doing. I made sure I knew in advance what I'd be doing every minute of those two hours, and in fact, every minute of my day. Beyond that, I employed several strategies to use my time effectively. One of those strategies was delegating. I said to my staff, "You do this, and I'll do that." And it worked.

Although this was an extraordinary situation, it illustrates that you can get whatever you want out of your day if you use time wisely. The key is to find the bull's nose. You do that by following some basic time management strategies.

Plan Your Day

If you take advantage of only one time management strategy, make it this one:

"Never begin the day until it is finished on paper." –Jim Rohn

Ideally, you should know at the end of each day what your schedule will be for the next day. (At the very least, you should plan your day as soon as you arrive in the morning.) If you know your schedule as soon as you arrive at work, you can hit the ground running. There's no doubt about exactly what you'll be doing, who you'll be seeing, and which problems you'll be solving. There's no start-up time–you begin your day at full speed. And because you've thought about your schedule, it more than likely incorporates plans needed to reach your longer-term goals. That's no small bonus.

Here's an example of my plan for a typical "in-town" day:

Daily Calendar for Troy

Monday
01/27/97

Reminder	SHEILA AND SUSAN: TAPES. TK
Reminder	DON'T FORGET SAN DIEGO PLANE TICKETS
Reminder	CALL JAY F
Reminder	FOLLOW-UP W/PHOENIX GROUP
Reminder	BRING VIP LIST TO CALL ON SD AGENT TRAINING SEMINAR
Reminder	HAVE SOMEONE PICK UP SHIRTS FRM CLEANERS FOR TRIP
Reminder	CALL LAURA B. RE: BOOK. 555-8167
7:30a 8:00a	STAFF MEETING 5 FOCUS GOALS. TK
8:30a 9:00a	JOYCE J, HERE, RE:R/A. 555-2531ⁱⁱTM W/F
9:00a 9:30a	JOHN G, HERE, R/A. 555-7298ⁱⁱCS W/F
9:30a 10:00a	BRAD&TRECIA W, HERE, N/B LIFE. 555-6012ⁱⁱ CS
9:45a 10:00a	RON B, PHN APPT, CLAIM?. 555-7234ⁱⁱCS W/F
10:00a 10:15a	MIKE&MARK M, HERE, BUY/SELL LIFE. CS W/F
11:00a 11:30a	DON&LOUSE R, HERE, A/R-LIFE RETIREMENT. 555-5827ⁱⁱW/F
11:30a 12:30p	LUNCH W/CRAIG K, DEPOT. WK 555-2009ⁱⁱ TM W/F
1:30p 2:00p	MARY M, HERE, N/B AUTO. WK 555-6673ⁱⁱ CS W/F
2:00p 2:30p	JOSEPH O, HERE, RA/LIFE.WK 555-9871ⁱⁱ CS W/F
3:00p 3:15p	JOHN U, PHN APPT, RE: DONATION. 555-2433
3:30p 4:00p	BOB F, HERE, N/B AUTO/HOME. 555-8873ⁱⁱ CS
4:30p 5:00p	KEN P, HERE, N/B HOME. 555-1286ⁱⁱSM
5:30p 6:00p	ROY J, HERE, R/A 555-7690ⁱⁱ TK
6:00p 6:30p	BEN C, HERE, N/B LIFE. 555-3654ⁱ8 TM
6:30p 7:00p	NO MORE APPTS!!!!

I couldn't even begin to get through all of that if I didn't plan. Planning keeps me focused on what's important, and puts me in control. The first thing I do when I arrive at my office is to take a look at my schedule and review my Five Focus Goals. If I need to make revisions, I make them as soon as I've walked in the door.

With a plan, I'm organized and mentally prepared for what's coming up. As I go through my day and problems arise, I don't get thrown for a loop. If it's necessary, I can make new priorities and rearrange my schedule intelligently. Planning doesn't tie me down. In fact, it frees me up to make better decisions about how best to use my time.

Banish Excuses for Not Planning

Most people in our industry don't spend time planning. They don't leverage their time. If planning is the key to control and if it's such a simple idea, why do so many agents ignore it? Here are six answers I frequently hear:

1. I don't have time to plan.
Believe it or not, this is the most common reason agents give for not planning. What they're really saying is that planning isn't as important to them as watching TV or reading the newspaper, or sleeping an extra fifteen minutes. They haven't placed a high enough value on planning. Maybe they

simply don't understand the genuinely terrific results that planning can make in their agencies.

2. I don't need to plan. Things are going well.
Agents who say this are content with the status quo, with letting life happen, rather than shaping and directing the events that make up the day. If you start your day with no plan, will you be reactive or proactive? By definition, you'll be reactive. And you won't be in control of your agency.

3. I already know what I have to do. Why take time to plan?
There are always routine tasks that need to be accomplished, which can sometimes eat up a significant chunk of your day. But what about the things that aren't so obvious? What about tasks that are the most important? If you truly ask yourself what you want out of life, what you want to accomplish with your career, many tasks will surface that are not a routine part of your day. For you to achieve your goals, a daily plan is necessary—even vital.

4. Planning doesn't work for me. I have too many interruptions.
You know what it's like to walk into your office in the morning, and before you can even take off your coat, someone notices you and says, "There you are! We need your help. It's urgent." Well, some days are just like that, and admittedly, interruptions can be a problem. But there are ways of turning them into opportunities rather than nuisances—if you seize control, which you do through effective planning.

If frequent interruptions are the rule rather than the exception in your agency, you need to plan in a way that will make the number of tasks, or the time needed to accomplish them, appropriate to the amount of time available. If your time is limited, break your tasks into smaller elements that can be squeezed between other activities.

5. I feel tied down when I have a long list of things I have to do.
No agent likes the idea of facing an overwhelming list of tasks. The solution, however, isn't to avoid planning, but to make your plans meaningful and effective. View a daily plan as your ticket to success. It's a friend, not a foe. Remember, planning puts you in control, and a by-product of control is freedom.

6. *I don't know how to plan properly.*

Welcome to the club. Most agents don't know how to plan effectively, and many give up after trying out an occasional "to do" list. Unfortunately, a "to do" list doesn't necessarily translate into effective planning. (In fact, nothing could be further from the truth.) But that doesn't matter. The best way to get better at planning is to practice!

Make a Habit of Planning

Advance planning is nothing extraordinary. All professionals organize their work this way. Think about your doctor, dentist, or attorney. When they walk into their offices, their day is planned. They know what they're going to do that day and who they're going to see. What they don't do is go into the office and start reacting to whatever is happening at the time. If they ran their office like that, they'd never be able to see their clients. The same holds true for all of us.

But developing an effective approach to planning has to start with discipline. There's simply no fooling around on this score. Planning has to become a habit. When it does, you'll experience a lot less stress. You'll also restore fun to your days at the same time you achieve your goals.

Don't let yourself get jittery at the notion of developing a habit. Remember, it only takes twenty-one days to change or create a habit, and having good habits will transform your life. This is something you have more control over than you might think, but if ever doubts creep in about whether the effort is worthwhile, just read the following:

Habit

I am your constant companion.
I am your greatest helper or your heaviest burden.
I will push you onward or drag you down to failure.
I am completely at your command.
Half the things you do, you might just as well turn over to me,
And I will be able to do them quickly and correctly.
I am easily managed; you must merely be firm with me.
Show me exactly how you want something done,
And after a few lessons I will do it automatically.
I am the servant of all great men
and, alas, of all failures as well.
Those who are failures, I have made failures.
I am not a machine,
though I work with all the precision of a machine
Plus the intelligence of a man.
–Author Unknown

Master Strategies to Use Your Time Effectively

Remember Dorothy from *The Wizard of Oz*? She got to where she didn't want to be when a tornado blew her off course. She got home to safety by simply clicking her heels together three times. If you're caught up in a Dorothy-like tornado, maybe what you need are some concrete, "click-thrice" strategies to manage your time.

Click on the following techniques, and try them out. Make them habits. The good news is that they work. The better news is that they aren't hard to master.

The Four-Hour Plan

How often do you actually start the day with a quiet cup of coffee, then hit the phone and watch the rest of the day unfold exactly as you planned? If you said "rarely" or "never," you're not alone. In fact, most agents are far more accustomed to working furiously all day, only to glance up at the clock at 4 p.m. with the sinking realization that they haven't gotten anything done.

They've been pulled by the bull's tail. The irony is that a lot of them probably started off by saying, "I'm going to do such-and-such today, this week, this month." They're blocking off too much time.

If this sounds like you, take heart. A simple, but enormously effective way around that kind of dilemma is to divide the day into manageable chunks of time. Try breaking the day into the four hours before lunch and the four hours after. Write down two or three things that you have to get done before lunch. If you have ten people to call, make sure you call them, or make sure you set your three appointments to do account reviews, or follow up on your Life Prospect List. Consider your day productive if you get two or three things done in each four-hour slot.

The four-hour plan works because when you tackle your day in smaller chunks of time, your schedule seems less overwhelming and therefore a lot more doable. The four-hour plan can actually vanquish that terrible villain of time–procrastination.

Try it. And enjoy your first four hours of work. And then your second.

Work Ahead

You can't control your day if you're always playing catch-up. And you'll always be playing catch-up if you don't get in the habit of working ahead. For as simple as that may sound, it's surprising how easy it is to find quite the opposite happening.

For example, too many agents literally wait for the mail to arrive to decide what to act on. Right away, they're working behind instead of ahead, and productivity goes right down the tubes. What's happened? They've opted to play defense. Personally, I far prefer to be on the offense.

I don't wait for the mail to come in to start my day. I generate mail so things will happen. That's being on the offense, and when you're on the offense, things that might go wrong turn out right.

Being on the offense can also spare you a lot of embarrassing situations when you're caught offguard, which can happen to anyone. For instance, if Mrs. Jones calls with an unexpected question, an agent on the defense might stammer something like, "Uh, I've got to look that up, Mrs. Jones. I just got back from lunch and my secretary is on her break, and I've got a client waiting for me in the lobby and, uh, can I call you back later?" An agent on the offense would simply say, "No problem, Mrs. Jones. We'll find out and call you back the moment we have an answer." In a sense, both agents are saying the same thing. But the agent on the defense sounds vague and uncertain while the agent on the offense sounds assured and professional. Who would you want to deal with?

No matter how you describe the tactic–being on the offense, taking the initiative, working proactively–it's all part of working ahead, not behind. Read on for some of the other components that'll keep you from playing catch-up.

Quickly Do What You Must

Working ahead is quickly doing the things you must do—no matter what. It's not necessarily doing everything at once.

For instance, I've got to take care of the people who bought policies from me because I promised them I would, and I will take care of them. That means if a client has filed a claim, one of my priorities is to call the person quickly. I don't "put it off" until after the next appointment; I do it before the next appointment. That's working ahead. That's time management.

On the other hand, is it likely that I'm going to settle the claim with that phone call? No, of course not. I promised I would take care of the client, and all it takes is a phone call to let the client know I care. I stop what I'm doing as soon as possible, make the call, and then continue with whatever I'm doing. It takes only a minute or two. It's that simple.

Do the Little Things Right

Working ahead means avoiding time wasters by doing the little stuff right, by tackling minor problems when they first crop up. That seems like a no-brainer, but in the rush of a busy day it's easy to put aside all the odd little problems that seem inconsequential. After all, there's always tomorrow, right?

Unfortunately, small problems have a nasty habit of snowballing into big ones, which can eat up whole chunks of your time and leave a lot of chaos in the process. They can leave you dancing with the wrong end of the bull again, and that's about the last thing you need.

The best strategy to avoid time wasters is to identify little problems early on–and then deal with them quickly and efficiently. I meet with my employees regularly. That way, I know when I have a problem, and I know it now instead of later when the amount of time it takes to solve the problem has grown way out of proportion.

Calendar

No one expects a carpenter to hammer a house together with thumbtacks and the heel of his shoe. It might be possible, but it would take him forever and the result wouldn't be very effective. The same might be said about the mechanics of your scheduling. If you're not using the right tools you're operating at a disadvantage that could cripple you, both in terms of time and efficiency.

The hammer you need is a calendar system that's accessible to everyone. In my office, we use a computerized calendar to plan schedules not only for me, but also for all the members of my high performance team. Nothing gets overlooked. The calendar even includes my off-hours schedule–evenings, early mornings, and Saturdays. And if I'm going out of town, I have appointments scheduled before I leave and after I come back. I guess you could say that our calendar system has pretty much turned my life into an open book–and thank goodness for it.

The system we have now is a far cry from what we used at the beginning. When we first started, we used an ordinary calendar book, not unlike what a dentist or a doctor might use. Unfortunately, people didn't always remember to put things in the book, and it got kind of confusing. It was also difficult for everyone to access the calendar when they needed it.

So, we went to a computerized system and developed some standards for using the calendar. Standards make sure everyone enters information in a consistent way, which eliminates a lot of potential errors. Here are the standards everybody follows when making entries:

Standardized Calendar Use

1. Entry should be in all caps

2. Must include:
   - Name of client
   - Location: HERE/THERE/PHONE APPT
   - Phone Number   Wk or Hm
   - Subject
   - Initials of Person Setting Appointment

3. Abbreviations
   - W/F Working File
   - R/A Review Appointment
   - H/O Homeowners
   - N/B New Business - Auto, Fire, Life, Comm'l.
   - A/R Auto Review

4. Include copy of calendar appointment printout.

5. Working files should have clearly written tab with appointment date.

6. An "*" should be place on appointments that have been confirmed.

Of course, knowing the "language" for making consistent entries is one thing. But just as important are getting the entries on the calendar promptly! That's a priority for all of us and everyone in the office works to make sure that when an appointment is set, the appointment is entered into the computer calendar immediately and completely. Every time, no exception!

The system works. We don't wind up with double booking, and

everyone has access to the calendar for my time, as well as for his or her own schedule.

It goes a long way toward strategic time management, and it certainly helps to prevent no-shows. Using the computerized calendar, the Agency Contact Representative is responsible for calling clients to confirm appointments. She calls the day before the appointment, just like your dentist does. If a client indicates that he or she won't be able to make the appointment, my Agency Contact Representative simply reschedules the person–immediately freeing up that particular time.

Bells and whistles don't go off when a spot opens up on the calendar, but because everyone has immediate, computerized access to the calendar, the hole is visible instantly. Most often, such holes are filled before the day is over.

With the computerized calendar I can also more easily deal with unexpected situations that might arise, simply because it helps me work ahead so efficiently. For instance, I can quickly glance at my schedule for the next day and review my upcoming appointments. If I see that an appointment just won't work out, I ask my Agency Contact Representative to alert the client and reschedule a new appointment at a more convenient time for all of us. When rescheduling is approached that way, changes don't become last-minute ordeals for the client or me. No one's time is wasted.

I'm additionally able to set aside time to attend to planning, goal setting, and office management tasks. I'd like to think I could do all of that on my own, and just carry around a schedule in my head. But that would be too much like building a house with thumbtacks and the heel of my shoe. I've got better things to do with my time.

Be Prepared

If too many of your days leave you feeling like a deer caught in the headlights of a car, think about the way you approach what you're doing. Chances are you simply haven't prepared for your day well enough. Maybe you haven't prepared at all. If that's true, you're not working ahead and your schedule can crush you.

You already know what one of the fixes is: Using a calendar that makes scheduling fast and efficient. But keeping up with the demands of a busy day calls for knowing the specifics of what's coming before they're in your face. There really is no simpler strategy for that than maintaining good client files. Files are key to effective preparation.

Strangely enough, however, the whole idea of files makes some people wince. I don't know why that should be. Files are the silent partners of information, ever ready to fuel you with the kind of data that can produce sales and generate the income you need for growth. Of course, that's only true of files that are kept current. Outdated files can be saboteurs and no one needs that. So in our office, we make it a priority to keep all files up to date and in a location where they can consistently be found.

Naturally, though, you have to be flexible with your filing strategy because what goes into a file cabinet also comes out for a variety of reasons, and it's not realistic to assume that every file will make its way back home in less than sixty seconds. For those occasions, we use "hold files," which help us find information we need in files that may be incomplete, in other offices, or in stacks on desks all over the office. Here's how that works: We place unfinished files ("working files") in a centralized location, prioritize our work, and schedule a specific time to complete the work. The file stays in the hold file until it's completed. Periodic reviews of hold files help us ensure that tasks are completed and the file is available when needed.

Why am I bothering with this much detail on files? Because they're essential for you when you prepare for an appointment. I don't go into any appointment without first making sure I have an up-to-date working file on my desk so that I don't have to get up in the middle of the appointment and look something up. Someone on my staff prepares the files the day before the appointment.

For example, if I'm going to be doing an account review, I want to be able to look inside the client's file folder and find printouts of computer screens with current policy amounts. If I'm going to be talking about a new life insurance program, my staff will have prepared some proposals and placed the appropriate literature in a folder. If I'm going to be talking about a commercial account, a questionnaire and a brochure will be placed in the file. Although I never show clients the proposals or the status screens from the computer, I want to know what the premiums will be for the client. But no matter what, we pre-do the folders for the next day.

Don't imagine for a minute that I work in the dark on this, and you don't have to either. A vital element of preparing ahead is creating an agency in which you can assign and delegate work. If your goal is to have ten appointments a day, you have to!

In my office, preparation isn't daunting because we all work together. We stay organized and cemented to the concept of a high performance team, which you may recall from Part I. So understand that as important as preparation is, I don't go at it alone. I don't have to do any paperwork. I don't have to call to confirm appointments. I don't have to follow up and make sure that an appointment was rescheduled. I don't do anything other than talk to the client, and assign and delegate the work created by the appointment. The files are always there for me and I can work ahead.

....

Troy's Bottom Line: Sleep well at night by getting a grip on your days with time management. All you need is a habit of planning.

....

MAKE THEM COME TO YOU!

By now, I'm accustomed to people looking at me like I've got two heads when I tell them that my typical workday includes ten appointments with clients—in my office, at my desk, where I'm surrounded with all the things I need to sell or discuss a policy. I understand the reaction, because let's face it, most folks would just as soon get a root canal as talk about their insurance needs.

At least that's what I used to think, back in the days when I frantically drove around town to meet with people in their homes or their offices. I spent more time in a hot car with my shirt sticking to my back than I did selling policies. It was madness! Worse, it wasn't building my business and it became abundantly clear that I had to alter my strategies—a lot.

You already know that one of the first changes I made was to hire an Agency Contact Representative, someone who could dial the phone forty times an hour and in the process secure ten appointments a day. But that wasn't enough. To physically meet with ten clients a day meant I had to get off the road. I had to make clients come to me, just as they do for lawyers, doctors and other professionals.

The key to doing that is first understanding that you are a professional, and that people will respect that. Obviously, though, what makes you a professional isn't just that you dress smartly and carry a briefcase with important-looking papers in it. Professionalism goes beyond that, right to the heart of your own philosophy. For me, the philosophy that drives my professionalism is that I run my business with a high ethical code and that I always, always give my clients the best policies I can, at the best prices I can.

I learned four things when I adopted this approach. One, clients will come in if you follow through with that kind of commitment. Two, they won't necessarily know what a swell person you are with an initial contact and they won't come in until they do. So you have to persuade them. Three, insurance is a numbers game and by calling enough people, I can reach more than enough interested people to make my business soar. Four, the ones I can't persuade are probably the ones I don't really want.

But First, You Have to Convince Them

All right. You know you're good. You know you operate ethically and with high standards. You know you'll offer clients the best deal you can for the coverage they need. So how do you get them to come in long enough for you to convince them of that, especially if they've never met you? How do you get them to carve out a chunk of their own busy schedule to accommodate the pace of your own?

It starts with your Agency Contact Representative, because the ACR is the person on the phone with the first opportunity to get a client's ear. Assuming you've hired an Agency Contact Representative who believes in what you do, and assuming you've given your Agency Contact Representative good scripts to use, the ACR will come through by giving clients–existing and potential–enough reasons to come in.

Your reasons might have to do with the kind of coverage you offer, how responsive your claims service is, what kind of prices you can make available, what new features you can provide, how quickly and efficiently you can get their insurance needs met, and so on.

Remember, too, that you're not bugging prospects at home. Your Agency Contact Representative is calling most of them at work, where they're already in a business mode and accustomed to dealing with professionals. That makes them more receptive to begin with, an important first step to getting them in the door–*your* door.

The All-Important Follow-Through

I wish I could tell you that once your Agency Contact Representative makes his or her initial pitch, clients would simply fall all over themselves to make an appointment for an office visit. Sometimes they do, but most often the ACR has to follow through with a second call, and maybe even a third or fourth. This is not a big deal, because with each subsequent call the client is getting to know your Agency Contact Representative as a familiar and pleasant voice. Their relationship becomes more personal, and personal means more committed. Frankly, a lot of clients begin to feel a sense of obligation. As busy as they may be, they don't want to say no to that nice person on the phone.

As the relationship develops between your Agency Contact Representative and the people she's calling, they'll also learn that you're not pushing anything on them. The call your Agency Contact Representative is making is not a high-pressured pitch. The ACR isn't going to try to make a sale. She's merely going to try and set up a circumstance in which you can make a sale—or just explain what you're all about. No one is asking clients or new prospects to hand over their credit card numbers or any kind of information that could be perceived as too familiar.

Besides, your Agency Contact Representative will have made it clear to clients and new prospects that the appointment itself won't eat up the better part of their morning or afternoon. With each call, she'll be assuring them that they can be in and out in twenty to thirty minutes. For clients who still struggle with finding a hole in their schedule, she'll walk them through enough scenarios until they find a time frame that's suitable for them and you.

Of course, it goes without saying that your Agency Contact Representative has to be diligent about keeping track of who needs to be called back for follow-through. There are a number of valuable systems for doing this, and I'll talk about what works for us later in "Market Your Market."

The One That Got Away

You're never going to connect with every client you initially target. You already know that. We all have stories about "the one that got away." And, partly, that's why you need to call so many to begin with. But on another level, not every potential client is the client for you.

To begin with, think about what kind of clients you really want.

For me, it's simple: I want the clients who already believe in insurance—not the ones who don't—and I want the clients who will respect my professionalism by making an appointment and coming in to see me. I don't have goals to reach the other ones. Someone else may find a market in them, but I haven't and for that matter, I really don't want to.

My philosophy on this stems from my own experience with the value of insurance. I'm a product of it. My father died when I was young, but fortunately he had a life insurance policy and my mother was able to raise five kids because of it. We weren't rich; far from it. But we weren't poor, either. The insurance did what it was supposed to do: It put food on the table, kept us in clothes, and helped us get through school. That's what insurance is all about, and that's why I believe in it.

So the ones that get away? I let them. I find the clients I know I can help. In turn, they respect me enough to come in and see what I can do.

....

Troy's Bottom Line: The clients you want are the clients who will come to you. Convince them of your professionalism and they'll be happy to–as many as ten a day.

....

RAMP UP WITH THE ANNUAL REVIEW

If you aren't achieving the success you want, it may be because you're ignoring one of the most critical opportunities you'll ever have to get people in front of you. I'm talking about the annual review, a scheduled conference held every year with each client to assess needs and make recommendations. For clients, the review is an opportunity to find out if they're properly insured. For you, it's much more. It's an absolute imperative. It's an imperative because it allows you to build relationships, educate clients, and discover unmet needs—which you can fill.

Having read all that, you might find it peculiar to hear what I have to say next: The annual review is not the time or place to sell insurance. It's the time to assess coverage in a relaxed atmosphere, which can lay a thoughtful foundation for later sales. Indeed, if you forgo a sales pitch during annual reviews, you'll be pleasantly surprised at how receptive your clients are to the recommendations that lead to sales later.

From my perspective, annual reviews make all the sense in the world but, incredibly, only twenty percent of all agents conduct them. That's not just a statistic—it's suicide! I know; that's a pretty strong word.

But it's true for three reasons:

- Your clients may not have the coverage they need. For example, the 1991 Oakland Hills fire in California taught us all a painful lesson. Far too many people who owned expensive homes were only fifty percent insured, a tragedy that could have been avoided entirely by the yearly review.

- You're forfeiting an exceedingly effective system for retaining business and increasing sales in a way that's comfortable and non-threatening to the client.

- The past does not equal the future. To retain business, you have to sell yourself and your company every year!

A Strategy with Multiple Benefits

There is no such thing as wasting time when you do annual reviews. For one thing, annual reviews fulfill the commitment you made to clients when you initially signed them up. If you're like most agents, you promised them you would get together every year to make sure their insurance stayed up to date and that they would always get the very best buy for their insurance dollar. That's no small commitment, and by following through on it you can achieve a number of desirable outcomes. Here are some of them:

If we could predict the future, we'd all be out of business. But we can't, and neither can your clients. What this means is that your clients' needs can easily change over the course of a single year, and changes often signal gaps in a client's program. Those gaps can be devastating, as evidenced by the Oakland Hills fire and any number of other disasters around the country. The way I see it, we have an obligation to not let that happen.

Don't forget, you're not in the insurance business simply to sell insurance; you're in it to help people. It's not likely that you'll forget that. It *is* likely that your good intentions can get lost in the shuffle of too many busy days. That's where the annual review shows its strength as a simple but effective tool. The minute after you conduct one, your client walks away satisfied that all is well, and pleased that you're looking out for his or her best interests. You get to go home knowing that you have.

The truth is, most people *do* have gaps in their insurance program. And you can't expect them to necessarily be savvy to those gaps. That's *your* job. It's why they signed up with you to begin with. *You* need to educate your clients on where the risks lie and how to cover them. If there's something new in the client's life—a home remodeling project, the birth of a child, or a major purchase like a boat, for instance–you have the perfect opportunity to talk about options.

Although you'll run into cases where no coverage exists at all (a family without life insurance, for instance), it's more likely you'll encounter people with *inadequate* coverage. And by the way, don't get rattled if you happen to learn that at the same time your client has a key policy with another agent or carrier. Of course, we know people carry policies with other companies, and that's okay. Where things can get tricky is when you try to assess the adequacy of the programs your clients purchased elsewhere. As likely as not, you'll have to try and ferret out what other policies they own, and with whom, and then figure out whether your clients are properly covered overall.

The annual review is the perfect forum for that kind of fact-finding mission, and it's perfectly fine if the review reveals that a client's insurance needs are indeed well met–even if much of it is with another company. I never feel that I've wasted my time just because no opportunities emerge. I'd rather have a client leave the review thinking, "Hey, I actually got something out of that, and the guy didn't try to sell me anything!" The policies you do have with any given client are something you want to protect.

The right perspective goes a long way toward retention.

Build a Relationship of Trust

Your clients may not have much of a choice when it comes to which local newspaper they'll subscribe to or which cable company will provide them with service. They're probably stuck with limited options, or maybe even *no* options. But people do have options when they're looking for insurance, and you can be sure that they're buying it from people they like and trust. Let them down or ignore them, and you can count on them going somewhere else.

Fortunately, the annual review provides clients with a clearly lit path to your door, because the review process allows them to get to know you better–and you to know them. It puts names to voices and faces, a terrific way to ensure the line of communication stays wide open. When communication stays open and flows both ways, trust builds. You get the opportunity to do one of the things you do best–make recommendations specifically tailored to the client.

Believe me, in a day and age when most people hardly know their next-door neighbors, building a familiar and trusting relationship is no small thing to your clients! You become not just a clerk who took their insurance application–the one and only time you've ever seen them–or the salesperson that's always trying to get them to buy more. You become a flesh-and-blood person who looks out for them, who truly does have their best interests at heart. When they're ready to purchase more coverage, which may or may not happen during the review itself, they won't be thumbing through the phone book to remember your name. They'll have it in their own address book. And they will come back to you.

Educate your Clients

People need insurance. It's a requirement for survival in the modern world. And people need information to make the best decisions about insurance for their families. So you must provide it. If it's not you, it'll be someone else, which is why it's important that you do a lot of explaining and educating in the annual review.

Again, the goal of the review is not to sell insurance, but to review coverage. That means educating clients about what products exist that they might need now or in the future. Prime examples are homeowners policies; better yet, life insurance. For instance, if I'm holding an annual review with a client who currently rents, I'll talk about homeowners policies. I'll say something like, "Let's look five or ten years down the road when your needs might be different than they are today. You rent now, but you'll probably own a home in the future."

The point is, I don't pull out brass knuckles when I do annual reviews. Pressuring clients to buy is not only a bad strategy, but the worst strategy. What I try to do instead is demonstrate that I have a full range of products and services. When the client is ready to move up to increased or new coverage, he'll turn to me. I will have educated him about options, and he'll know that I can deliver on them. And if he's got other coverage elsewhere, the time I took to educate him will be rewarded if he becomes jaded with that other company.

Retain Business

It's a safe bet that you worked hard to build the client base you have. Depending on its size, you might regard it as a terrific launch pad for real growth, the kind of growth you've always dreamed about. But scrambling after new clients won't do you a bit of good if you lose the ones you already have, and losing them can be a lot easier than getting them.

In fact, the only way to achieve real growth in your agency is to retain your current clients through careful, thoughtful—and repeated—attention. If you think not, consider this: In one study my agency did, we learned that people need to be contacted three to five times before they're likely to buy from you, before they'll even establish that all-important beginning relationship with you. That upfront work represents a fair amount of time and no small measure of commitment on your part. So why on earth would you let those hard-earned clients walk out the door by overlooking their needs later? Clearly, you don't dare!

Once again, there's no better way to make sure that doesn't happen than by conducting annual reviews. It's a regular "check-up," your insurance against the ugly prospect of hungry competitors just waiting to prey on your clients. Don't let them!

Gather Information for Later Sales

Information is king. You know that intuitively, but if you're not holding annual reviews then you're forfeiting a golden opportunity to gather it. In an annual review, you're face to face with a client who already knows and trusts you. You've got a receptive person in your chair. Can you think of a better time to mine for information that can lead to future sales? (And an efficient agent will give that information directly to his or her Agency Contact Representative for follow-up!)

I'm not suggesting you have to ride into an annual review like a stealth plane pilot. Nor should you blast in like a bomber pilot. If you've designed annual reviews to be comfortable, non-threatening sessions, information will flow easily and naturally from it. Information can come from a casual comment, or from more specific policy discussions.

As I said earlier, identifying gaps in coverage presents a clear opportunity for future sales—and notice, please, my emphasis on the word "future." Remember, your goal during an annual review is not to make sales on the spot. On the other hand, when such an opportunity shows itself, don't wait too long to get moving on what you've learned. I usually try to schedule an appointment to address gaps right away.

The offhand comment, the casual aside, the conversation about looking toward the future . . . those are all great ways to get information that can build future sales. But a huge advantage of the annual review—maybe the biggest—is the open door you'll have for the ultimate: expiration dates on all your clients' policies! And make no mistake, those expiration dates–or "x-dates"–are gold. Get enough of them and over time you can build a dynamic database that won't cost you a dime. Best yet, those x-dates are fast slides into new policies that you might otherwise never get a shot at.

I won't kid you. It's a lot of effort to pry loose x-dates, but they're essential for building your agency. Think about it. If you do four annual reviews a day and get two x-dates from each, that's eight x-dates a day, or forty a week–a mother lode of opportunity! And those are good x-dates with people you already know.

After jotting down the x-dates for a client (I use the "Household Update Sheet" in Appendix B), I tell the person that my Agency Contact Representative will call to set up an appointment as the expiration date draws near. With that kind of preparation, the chances of converting at least some of the x-dates into applications are not just good, they're excellent.

And to think that the first step into this gold mine of opportunity is so easy. Telephone the client and ask him to come in for an annual review!

The Nuts and Bolts of Annual Reviews

There really isn't any magic or mystery to annual reviews. But that's not to say that what you do before, during and after them doesn't make a difference. Even seemingly minor elements of an annual review can matter in a big way, so they all call for a thoughtful approach. The strategy I've found effective for years is about as simple as they get. Here it is:

Scheduling

By now, you'll hardly be surprised to hear that if you want to schedule annual reviews with your clients—and you do—then you've got to reach out to the client. Trust me, clients won't just pop in to put their names on your book, no matter how terrific you are. Besides, don't forget that most of them won't even realize that their coverage probably calls for improvement.

To get those clients scheduled, your best bet is to assign your Agency Contact Representative to seek appointments with them. Even if you never hire an Agency Contact Representative, make it a priority to telephone clients yourself to set up annual reviews. They're just that important!

In our office, we use a very simple system to help us schedule annual reviews regularly. It looks like this:

Month	Appointments scheduled for clients with last names beginning with:
January	AB
February	CD
March	EF
April	GH
May	IJ
June	KL
July	MN
August	OP
September	QR
October	ST
November	UV
December	WXYZ

We're upfront about reviews, and we even give our review schedule to all new clients. At the same time, we explain how we do the review and why it's important. Sure, sometimes you'll encounter resistance when you actually follow through and telephone a client to ask for the appointment, especially if it's the client's first annual review. But persistence and good sales techniques won't let you down. In fact, I've found that my battle is half done by the time clients come in. Why? Simply because I've taken the time to lay the right foundation; I've pre-sold them on the value of the annual review. When they walk in the door, they've had time to think about it and they're receptive to what we're trying to do. They know I'm not about to give them a snow job.

Preparing

If you've taken the time to persuade your clients that it's important for them to come in for an annual review, don't botch things by being unprepared for them. Be ready with a packet of information that you've already familiarized yourself with. Inside the packet, which should be at your fingertips throughout the review, make sure you've included basic information about the client, such as the client's age, size of house, occupation and so on. If the basics are readily accessible, you'll be able to quickly field questions about insurance discounts if queries should come up.

For me, it's easiest to approach the prep work in the morning before the day gets rolling. I take about ten minutes per appointment to get a mental picture of each appointment. I review each customer file, assess coverage needs and opportunities, and create an agenda for the upcoming appointment. Your own strategy may differ, and that's fine. Just make sure you don't put yourself in a position where you wind up fumbling for information while the client is sitting at your desk. That "nice to see you" grin on his face won't stay there long if you do.

You may have noticed that I'm not big on "rules" as such. I much prefer strategies and suggestions. But when you're conducting annual reviews, there really are two ironclad rules to follow, and both are vital:

- **Never, never sell during the review.** I know I said it before, but I'm saying it again because the temptation to sell may be great. But fight it off. Instead, use the review time to go over coverage and gather information. Talk concepts–the purpose of insurance, which risks to cover and which to ignore–not cost. Your primary question should be, "Do you have enough coverage?" Save the selling for later, in a different interview.

- **Keep it short.** Don't let annual reviews stray over half an hour, and try to keep them closer to twenty minutes. Any time you go longer than twenty to thirty minutes, you risk losing the client's attention. If you identify areas in a client's insurance program that beg for additional attention, schedule an appointment for later. Believe me, the client will respect you for respecting his or her time.

What actually happens from the moment a client walks in your door to the moment the client leaves is entirely up to you. You have to control the situation, and you can do that without appearing rushed or brusque. In fact, if you've prepared in advance, you won't be rushed. You'll feel relaxed, and that's a feeling that you'll project to your client. Both of you will be operating from the same comfort zone.

I start annual reviews with pleasantries, the usual kind of mild conversation that might deal with the weather or a sports game . . . that sort of thing. Pleasantries are an agreeable way to break the ice, to make clients relax. But I don't linger there long.

After a minute or two, I use an "opener" to lead clients into conversation about insurance in a general sort of way. I might say, "Let's talk about what a fire policy does," or, "Let's talk about what it means to have life insurance." (The conversation might just as easily center on auto or commercial insurance; the point is to ease the client into a business discussion in a non-threatening way.)

Usually, I talk first about my clients' auto insurance and explain available options for upgrading coverage if appropriate. Next I talk about their homeowners insurance. If they have it with me, I review their coverage and make suggestions to save them money or improve coverage. If they don't have it with me, I tell them what a great product we offer and I let them know I'll be following up with a call at renewal time to see if my agency can take care of that policy also. Remember that the annual review is all about opportunities that can pave the way for growth and I'd be foolish to pass on whatever opportunities present themselves.

But I never, never try to sell during a review. I keep my focus on building our relationship. I want to cement my clients to the agency so they'll never even consider anyone else. If I unearth an area of one of my client's insurance programs that need further attention, I simply set another appointment to focus on that specific issue. That appointment would take about thirty minutes. Because I don't try to sell in the annual review, I can get it done quickly.

Let's take life insurance, for example. If I'm not the client's life insurance agent, I don't say, "Hey, how's your life insurance?" That's simply not professional. Instead, I say, "Hey, I know I don't cover your life insurance, but I need to ask you a couple of things for the file because your family thinks of me as your insurance agent." Then I ask how much life insurance the client's job provides. Next, I ask what additional life insurance the person carries. Ninety-five percent of the time it doesn't amount to much, and the client frequently recognizes that himself when he adds it up. In fact, more often than you might imagine, it's the client who will actually say something like, "That's not very much, is it?" And the conversation about life insurance begins.

The beauty of this approach—reviewing policies, not selling them—is that clients wind up asking me what I can offer, whether it's life insurance they're interested in or any other type of coverage. It's a fabulous opening for me to show them that I provide a variety of products that can be tailored to their needs.

I'll admit that the temptation to launch into a full-scale sales mode can be daunting. Actually, it can almost be overwhelming. But I hang tough. I answer questions, make key points, and tell them my Agency Contact Representative will call to arrange an appointment so I can explain the options in more detail.

It's at this point that I make sure to emphasize one of the most important and powerful messages that you need to get across at the annual review: Having insurance with one agent prevents gaps. It also prevents unnecessary coverage and premiums. This isn't as self-serving as it may sound to someone outside our industry. At the very least, if you take care of all the insurance needs for your clients, your clients save time because they only have to deal with your agency. It's one-stop shopping and of the best kind. But more importantly, you help your clients prevent the kinds of disasters that inadequate coverage can allow. And you also help them save money, sometimes quite a bit.

It's been my experience that most fire and casualty agents have a thing about life insurance, and frankly, I don't get it. To me, life insurance is no different than the rest of the products we sell. I don't emphasize life insurance any more than any of the other lines of insurance. But I don't emphasize it any less.

Here's my take on this: I'm in the business to sell insurance and make sure my clients are protected on every level. I want them to feel secure in knowing that all of their needs can be taken care of by the Troy Korsgaden Insurance Agency. Making sure my clients have life insurance–and the right amount of life insurance–is part of that. It's part of the job of every member of my high performance team. So during an account review, if a client has life insurance with us, we'll review the coverage to make sure it's still the correct amount. If the client doesn't have life insurance with us, I tell him or her what fine products we have, and I'll try to set an appointment for a future date. If the client and I can't come up with a date, you can be sure I'll give the name to my Agency Contact Representative. The Agency Contact Representative will take over. He or she will start contacting the client to set a time to review life insurance options.

A commercial account review works the same way as personal

insurance. If we currently insure a particular business, we'll go over the coverage and make sure nothing has changed since the previous year. If we don't have the commercial account, I find out when the policies renew and let the client know I need to review those policies before that date. But I never, ever try to sell them at that time. Again, this is the time to build trust and confidence in the agency. I'll take down the information I need for future sales, and finish up with the client by advertising a little—talking about the benefits of my company and my agency.

Incidentally, the annual review isn't over when the client walks out the door. It doesn't end until I've passed along whatever information I obtained during the review to my ACR for follow-up on appointments and x-date calls.

One More Time with Feeling . . .

I can't stress enough the importance of the annual review. Vow to yourself you'll contact your clients once a year to review coverage, especially life insurance coverage, and then do follow through.

I promise you, after clients experience one review they'll be more receptive to future meetings. They'll know they don't have to endure a hard sell that makes them uncomfortable. They didn't get that over the phone when the appointment was set, and they won't get it at your desk on the day of the appointment.

What they *will* get is knowledge and help. They'll have learned that an annual review really is a forum to put their insurance programs in perspective. And how refreshing for them! Finally, it's someone giving–not taking.

Here's another promise: Because annual reviews expose areas of risk that need coverage, if you schedule enough reviews, then show some patience and work for the sales in subsequent meetings, you'll soon be doing more business than you dreamed possible. And to think that eighty-percent of agents are waiting for someone to walk through the door! With annual reviews, you'll be so busy you'll wonder what took you so long to get started.

Troy's Bottom Line: Annual reviews are the bread and butter of a successful agency. Schedule them daily and they'll feed new growth without you even making a sales pitch.

A RIGHT-TO-THE-POINT APPROACH

Unless you don't get out much, you've undoubtedly been on the receiving end of a business conversation that seemed to go on endlessly without taking you anywhere. You know the feeling. At first, you smile and nod pleasantly. Then you start fidgeting with paperclips and glancing furtively at your watch. You try to hold the smile, but all you really want to do is leap out of your chair and scream, "Please! Just cut to the chase and let's get on with it!"

Sometimes, it's clients who do that to you. But if you're not careful, it can be you doing it to them as well, and eating up their time that way can be deadly. Either way, the most effective method for getting and giving value time is a "right-to-the-point" approach.

I try to look at situations as if I were the consumer. I know when I visit a stockbroker, talk to a real estate agent, or see a doctor, I don't want to be kept waiting and I sure don't want to listen to a bunch of fluff. My attitude is, "Get to the point! I'm a busy guy." But I can't trot that attitude out if I don't practice it in reverse. My clients are busy people, and I know that they appreciate a "right-to-the-point" approach; it's been demonstrated to me time and again.

Believe it or not, it's not only acceptable, but it's downright professional to be so busy that you can only spend a limited amount of time with your clients. People tend to prefer dealing with professionals who strike them as busy, important, and successful. Handled correctly, offering them a limited amount of time can actually make them feel special, and they'll understand that you don't have time to look at every picture in Grandma's brag book.

Now obviously, the last thing you want to do is blow your clients off–that's fatal. But a right-to-the-point approach illustrates that you value their time, and they'll respond to that. They'll know they're getting what they came for and that your agency is organized to serve them efficiently without sacrificing quality.

So how do you pull this off without offending anyone? How do you find the balance that will meet your clients' objectives and your own?

Let's talk strategy . . .

Implement the 30-Minute Appointment

Get your clients in and out in thirty minutes or less! That may not sound like much time, but if you're prepared, stay focused, and know what you want to accomplish, thirty minutes is plenty—and no one's eyes will glaze over.

I'm not suggesting that you operate your agency with a fast-food mentality. The minute we resort to drive-through windows, we're all in trouble. But if you work ahead so that you're prepared for your appointments and you have an agenda when clients come in, you will get them in and out in thirty minutes.

That said, there is a certain mentality you need to bring to thirty-minute appointments. And that mentality is this: You're there to serve your clients, not to marry them.

For instance, when a client walks through my door, I say, "Hi, how are you?" —and we get down to business. If we want to be friends, we can go to lunch and split a pizza. We can join the Y together. But when clients come in for an appointment, they're not there to chitchat. They're there to talk about their insurance. So sure, I serve up a minute or two of pleasantries. But I don't mix work and play. I make sure I have a thoughtfully prepared presentation and I deliver it in a way that won't confuse them. I'll tell you more about strategies for effective presentations in the last chapter.

Of course, once your agenda is completed, you can't merely pop off your chair and say, "Thanks! I've got to go now!" No one would view that as anything but what it is–rude.

So how do you respectfully usher someone out of your office without sounding abrupt? Simple! Just stand up and start walking to the door. Keep talking while you've moving. It's not impolite and you won't offend your client. For that matter, the walk-and-talk strategy is a lot better than chewing up time with awkward and aimless conversation, hoping the appointment will end gracefully.

Ninety percent of the time, when you just stand up to power down your appointments, your clients will rise with you. On those occasions when you can't seem to disengage comfortably or when you know in advance you're about to see a client who tends to go on and on, don't panic. Have a policy in place for your staff to ring your phone in twenty to thirty minutes. When push comes to shove, a jangling telephone can do wonders.

Frankly, I simply couldn't be effective if I let appointments slide beyond thirty minutes. For one thing, the thirty-minute appointment literally doubles the number of appointments I can do in a day. For another, it still leaves me time to call people back, to do follow-up dictation, or maybe follow through by assigning the work to someone else. Try it. You won't be sorry you did.

Make Buddies with Your Telephone–Briefly

I admit it. I've been known to glare at my phone like it was some living, breathing human being, and I've done it on more than one occasion. I bet you have, too. That's because for all its puny size, the telephone is an unbelievably domineering machine that shrieks for attention. Given half a chance, it would probably grow legs and follow us all to the bathroom. As for its cellular cousin–well, I don't have to tell you how much stealthier *that* character is.

Clearly, when it comes to our phones, we need the upper hand. I've tried a number of tactics over the years, and I haven't found one yet that's better than buddying up to the darned thing–briefly. It's part of a right-to-the-point strategy, and every bit as important as knowing how to ease your clients out the door at the end of a thirty-minute appointment.

For me, part of getting that upper hand means avoiding the standard knee-jerk reaction to a ringing telephone to begin with. Truthfully, someone else on your staff can probably handle a lot of the calls that come in for you just as effectively as you can yourself. And in most cases, as long as the caller is getting attention and answers, he'll be satisfied. Besides, as your agency grows, you want your whole office to be accessible, not just you!

Beyond that, you can almost always be faster and more effective by returning a phone call than you can be by responding to one on the spot. If you have even a glimmer of what the caller wants, you can save both of you time by collecting the information you'll need before you call the person back.

When you get down to it, the phone is just another business tool, no more, no less. The only thing that makes it more important than a paperclip is what's attached to it—a human voice. And that's the bottom line. If the voice on the other end is a client, you're really facing the same dilemma that you do when a client is in your office. For that reason, your best bet is to approach a telephone conversation the same way, but in a lot less time.

Start by vowing to avoid "chitchat." You don't have the advantage of being able to read body language like you do in a face-to-face encounter, but you can "read" the gaps in a conversation. Don't rush to fill them! If it helps, simply pretend there's a meter on your phone, and that the meter is a lot more expensive than any long-distance call. Avoiding chitchat doesn't mean you have to cut people off. It just means you have to bring the same savvy to phone conversations as you do to conversations in your office.

Having an agenda is likewise every bit as important for telephone calls as it is for face-to-face appointments. If you're the one making the call—and you should be doing a lot more of that than spontaneously grabbing up the phone—be prepared. For instance, if I'm calling someone I know is a big talker, I write down what I need from that person before I even dial the phone. I might have a list that says, "need license number," "need registration number," "need appointment to deliver policy," or "need date when to call back on life insurance." Thinking ahead before dialing helps me define my agenda and be prepared for an efficient phone call. It puts me in charge.

Since time truly is money, the best phone call is a brief phone call. When I sense that the person on the other end is aiming in the other direction, I pull out two strategies to bring the conversation to a close:

- I stand up! Yes, right there at my desk. I don't know if there's a scientific explanation for it, but my voice changes and the tone of the conversation changes with it. The caller can sense the difference, and the conversation draws to a close. Simple, but effective.

- I use some good-natured humor to cut the conversation short, and follow up later by calling back early in the morning, late at night, or maybe from my car.

Remember that the telephone only seems like a living, breathing entity. Show it who's boss right from the start and it'll behave more like the business tool that it is.

Don't Waste Time In Between

If you're going into your days with a right-to-the-point approach that means you're busy virtually all of the time. You have regularly sched-uled thirty-minute appointments, and you're dealing with phone calls that you control. It seems like a lot–and it is. But believe it or not, once you've mastered those techniques you'll actually have some time to spare, so don't put your feet up on the desk yet.

The time in between is gold. It's what allows you to accomplish those "working ahead" tasks I discussed earlier. Whether the gaps between appointments are short or long, it's absolutely to your advantage to leap right on them. Indeed, it's that "in between" time that gives you room for setting goals, formulating strategies, refining your marketing plans, reading important correspondence or industry journals, and, of course, working on developing your staff into a high performance team.

Deal With the Unexpected Effectively

Up until now, I've pretty much described a best-case scenario for your days. You get a steady string of clients in front of you, they stay for their prescribed thirty minutes, you handle only necessary phone calls and you handle them quickly. In between, you create goals and map out a plan that'll take your agency to superstar status.

Sounds swell, and it is swell–once you get past the interruptions, those nasty time thieves that can take a chunk from your day the size of the Grand Canyon. Of course, that's only if you let them.

When interruptions arise–and our business is full of them–staying in control is critical. You do that best by limiting the unexpected, and by handling the unexpected well.

Limit the Unexpected

If you keep a good calendar and scheduling system, you already know a lot about limiting the unexpected, because a proper system is the most powerful strategy you'll ever find for doing away with no-shows and double-booking. Clients with appointments scheduled in advance will arrive on time because your Agency Contact Representative has been trained to call them the day before.

If you've got any reservations at all about "bugging" people in advance, just think of it this way: Your doctor, dentist and attorney inevitably call to confirm your appointments, and you're probably grateful for the reminder. Well, you're a professional, too, and people will be just as receptive to getting your reminder calls. In the process, you'll put a lid on one of the biggest offenders of wasted time.

Handle the Unexpected Well

No matter how good you are, and no matter how finely tuned your scheduling system, unexpected situations will still come up. I'm not talking about calamities like earthquakes. Those fall into a different class altogether.

But the clients who stroll in unannounced, the people who walk in off the street looking for directions, the folks who call and insist on talking to you right now—those are the kinds of interruptions that can put a kink in even the best laid plans if you don't know how to handle them quickly and efficiently. Here are the ABCs for doing just that:

• Keep your files updated, and know where to find them. What sounds like a quick question at first blush can turn into a long search if you don't.

• Make sure your staff works together as a high performance team, and that they all understand your priorities and know what your schedule is. Let them help you control your immediate environment!

• Get someone pleasant to screen your calls.

Elsewhere in this book, I've talked at length about the first two components of handling the unexpected well. They work! But the notion of having someone screen your calls merits some further discussion.

First of all, don't worry that having a screener will appear rude to clients or potential clients. Most people are accustomed to having a receptionist or someone other than you pick up calls on an office line, especially in a professional setting. (In fact, people are so resigned to automated answering systems by now that they're surprised and delighted to hear a human voice on the other end of the phone at all!)

Secondly, the truth is you are too busy to handle every single call that comes in, and you may well not be the best person to handle all of them, anyway. Remember, one of the key objectives for growth is to "replace yourself" with good people in functions that otherwise serve only to distract you from your major goal: having clients in front of you. So delegate the responsibility of answering the phone to someone personable who will know how best to route calls.

I'm fortunate to have someone at my front desk who's fantastic in finding out what clients need and getting them transferred to the right person (which may not be me). By screening calls, clients don't get bounced around needlessly, nor do cobwebs grow around their telephone handsets while they wait for answers.

Of course, every once in a while, a client calls and only wants to speak to me—and he or she should be able to speak to me. You want to make people feel like you're always accessible, even if you're not, or at least not at that moment. The only way to do that is to make sure you have a good screener. A screener will get the messages to you that you need to get, and not disrupt you with the messages you don't need. Later, when you've got some of that "in between time" I talked about earlier, you can take a moment to create an agenda for the call and get back to the person. You maintain control of your time, and it's the screener who helps you do that.

It's all part of keeping the unexpected at bay, and handling the unexpected that you can't keep at bay in a smooth, efficient manner. And if you've got a solid plan for doing that, you'll ride the rails instead of being thrown off track. At the end of a day, your internal stress meter will thank you for it.

....

Troy's Bottom Line: When you operate with a "right-to-the-point" approach, you get value time and you give it. Clients will make it in and out of your office in thirty minutes or less and you'll nip interruptions in the bud.

....

MARKET YOUR MARKET

You're probably familiar with the mind-numbing question that goes something like this: If a tree falls in a forest and there's no one there to hear it go down, did it make a sound? I don't know how you weigh in on this, but I'd sure like to think that not only did the tree make some noise, but that someone saw it move as well.

Marketing is kind of like that. It has to make some noise. You have to make some noise. (And you also want your tree to grow, not fall!)

Well, trees aside, when you set out to achieve your goals for business growth, you dare not forget to incorporate some fundamental marketing tactics. This is genuinely a case of "if you snooze, you lose," because even a superb Agency Contact Representative and a highly motivated agency staff can't come to the rescue if you don't market aggressively and consistently.

Fortunately, getting the word out doesn't have to be daunting if you attack it with a simple, but powerful, two-pronged method: internal marketing and external marketing. Each has its own reason for being, and therefore its own approach. But together, they're the framework for defining targets and strategies that increase sales. And I guarantee they'll make you some noise.

Market Internally

Internal marketing is nothing more than targeting current clients to expand the types and coverage of insurance you provide to them. But for all its simplicity, it offers terrific advantages, particularly for agents with an established client base.

In terms of retention, internal marketing helps you hang onto clients by strengthening your relationship with them. In terms of operations, internal marketing helps you boost sales volume. Consider, for instance, how much more readily you can sell to and service 1,000 clients with four policies in each household than to sell to and service 4,000 clients with only one policy in each household. Who can argue with that kind of math, right?

Not only that, but by internal marketing you set up a situation for new leads. Let's face it, your existing clients are great pipelines to new business. If they like what you offer and they're pleased with the professionalism you bring to the relationship, they'll tell their friends and neighbors. That's the greatest kind of grapevine in the world.

If you adopt a couple of consistent strategies for internal marketing, you'll experience a parallel in consistent growth. Try these tactics out for size:

Conduct Annual Reviews

Annual reviews, scheduled conferences held annually with all your clients, are critical forums for talking about gaps in their insurance coverage and for making recommendations that'll fix those gaps. They do a lot more than that as well, and they're crucial to the success of any agency. In fact, annual reviews should be the leading strategy in your internal marketing arsenal.

I could go on and on about the enormous value of annual reviews, but it seems I already did. You'll find expanded discussion in an earlier chapter called "Ramp Up with the Annual Review."

Market Additional Lines of Insurance to Existing Clients

The beauty of an existing client base is how expandable it is. The tragedy is how often agents overlook it. I hope you're not one of them, because the folks currently in your file folders are already receptive to you. That makes them tremendous targets for specific, additional lines of coverage that you can provide. It's another basic strategy for internal marketing.

For me, two approaches have generally proved successful in carrying out this strategy. The first is to simply aim for an appointment with an existing client to discuss an additional line of insurance. The second is to provide a client with information on a line of insurance that the person doesn't already carry with you, then try to set up an appointment.

Neither approach happens automatically, of course. You have to go into them with initiative, organization, consistency, and an effective pitch. You also need someone skilled to set up the appointment, which is where your Agency Contact Representative comes into play, or an outside firm that specializes in setting appointments or following up with letters. You already know how high I am on using my own Agency Contact Representative. But an equally viable option is to use an outside company to enhance your effort.

It is all about consistency, really. Whether you try to sell new lines of insurance to existing clients on your own or through an outside firm, consistency is a critical ingredient if you want your books to show new business from old clients.

Create Specific Projects

One of the best internal marketing tools you'll ever find is sitting right outside your office door. I'm talking about your staff, those skilled employees you've turned into a high performance team. Who will ever be better motivated than they to help develop new ideas? Who will ever understand the nuance of your day-to-day operation better? If you involve them in your efforts, together you can brainstorm your way into ideas that translate into new income.

What can come up? Actually, just about anything. Energetic brainstorming sessions might prompt you to target homeowners with high liability limits for umbrella policies. Or maybe they'll lead you to new ideas on how to add towing coverage to auto policies that don't have it. The potential is high, because even the germ of a new idea can evolve into something way beyond what you could develop on your own or through an outside service agency.

Just make sure you whip out a pencil when new ideas emerge.

You might think you'll remember them, but ideas can evaporate like early morning dew if you don't get them on paper. Later, once you've fleshed out the particulars of an idea and produced an actual plan for turning them into a marketing strategy, create an in-house list to call on. Have one or two specific projects that you and your staff are working on at all times. You'll cover a lot of ground that way and in the process, you'll grow a lot of new coverage.

Market Externally

External marketing is the flip side of internal marketing. It's reaching outside your existing client base to attract new business. Do it well and you'll drive precisely the kinds of clients you want to your door. Approach it haphazardly and you'll spin your wheels without leaving a trace of rubber to show for the effort.

External marketing doesn't have to be scary, complicated or expensive. If you approach it the same way you approach internal marketing, you'll never have to stray far from your comfort zone, because both rely on the same fundamentals: initiative, organization, consistency, and an effective pitch. What sets the two efforts apart is strategy. Here are the external marketing strategies that work for me:

X-Dating

No two ways about it. Expiration dates on policies are lightning rods for new business. But you can't just put them on your roof and wait for a good storm. First you have to find them, and then you have to show some initiative in using them.

Getting expiration dates, or "x-dates," is most readily accomplished by purchasing or creating pre-qualified lists of potential clients. There are a number of sources available, and plenty of outside companies will be thrilled to step up to the plate and take on your challenge. In fact, for new agents starting out, buying lists may be the most reasonable and expedient alternative. At any event, once you have those lists, you simply call from them and gather information regarding renewal dates for various lines of insurance.

And don't forget, if you're creating or expanding x-date lists of your own, don't overlook what you can learn directly from existing clients. If they don't hold all of their policies with you, find out where the holes are. Try to learn when their "outside" policies will come up for renewal.

They're fair game for conversion to your agency!

The next step is to simply put the information into your own follow-up system, which brings the data back to you just before the insurance is up for renewal. Your Agency Contact Representative can leap on that information to do what he or she does best—set appointments that'll get people in front of you.

Acquire and Use "Introduction" Lists

We could not do business without a continual infusion of information. In our industry, that's an absolute. But not all information is equal and when it comes time to seek new clients your Agency Contact Representative must have a steady stream of valid "introduction lists." Resourceful Agency Contact Representatives eventually become great at developing their own lists, but especially in the beginning it's crucial that you provide them. And tossing a fat phone book on his or her desk won't do the trick. Phone books are way too general and ultimately, counterproductive.

What you're after are introduction lists that are made up of qualified, potential clients. If you're just starting out, consider buying lists from outside companies, a tactic I mentioned earlier. But don't aim to rely on them alone, or for the long haul. Your goal, along with your Agency Contact Representative, should be to develop your own introduction lists as well.

Nothing is sweeter than proprietary information. Once you have a database that contains viable names and numbers, you're a big step ahead of your competition. Besides that, you'll find that your costs can actually go down while your business growth spirals up.

You'd be surprised at how many resources there are to tap for your own introduction lists. Some might be generated from your associations in the field. Others might be created from church directories, chamber of commerce lists, reverse directories, new subdivisions, newspapers and more. Get creative!

Create a Hot List

Potential clients don't walk around with big "C's" on their forehead for ready identification. Still, it's amazing how many of them are out there, and it's even more amazing how many of them are people who might already be favorably inclined to do business with you. Some might be referrals. Some might be casual acquaintances. They might even be your butcher, baker or candlestick maker—folks you've chatted up within or outside of an insurance context. The point is, more of them than you might think are "hot" candidates for either new insurance or an additional line of insurance with you. They ought to be going down on a list.

I keep a current list of about one hundred current and potential clients who I want for a particular line of insurance. Often these people are "Centers of Influence," something I'll discuss shortly. But no matter where or how I find candidates, I keep their names and numbers on a "hot list" with me in my schedule book, and I look at it daily. I seem to gravitate toward these people, and they seem to gravitate toward me. It makes for an easy and comfortable relationship, and when it comes time to talk about insurance, staying focused isn't difficult.

Naturally, people on my hot list don't always turn into "instant" sales. If that were true, I probably could have retired by now. (Not that I want to!) But I find that I do end up insuring almost everyone who goes on that list. After a sale to one of them, I check off the name and replace it with a new one.

Following is the kind of format I use for a hot list.

Hot List

Ask for a Life Appointment Today!

Date	Name	Phone	Appt.	Comment
12/9/97	Robert H	555-9981	1/24	Add on life police, likes cash value
1/15/98	Brad W	555-6012	1/27	Has term policy
1/18/98	Ken P	555-1286	1/27	Add on personal life insurance. Has business with us.
1/22/98	Keith K	555-2356	2/3	Add'l business insurance. $500K
1/22/98	Dr. Joe M	555-7620	2/8	Estate Planning. Needs an add'l $1M
1/24/98	Don R	555-7031	2/7	Has not increased insurance in 3 years
1/24/98	Ben C	555-3654	1/27	Needs personal life ins. Has business w/us

Your own hot list probably won't start off with a hundred people on it. Don't worry that it won't be successful if it doesn't. Try a hot list with ten to twenty names until you get comfortable with the concept. When you see how valuable even a modest hot list can be and how easy it is to develop, yours will almost seem to grow of its own accord.

Launch a Referral Reward Program

You'll be happy to know that some of the best strategies for external marketing are also the most elementary. Case in point: a referral reward program. It's exactly what it sounds like. When an existing client sends someone new your way, you need to say "thanks."

A verbal acknowledgment is nice, of course. Better, though, is some kind of thoughtful gesture that shows active participation on the part of your agency. That gesture doesn't need to be more than a thank-you card. Or it could be as elaborate as a gift certificate for lunch in a fine restaurant.

The size of the gesture isn't as important as what it says about you. To the client who made the referral, the gesture underscores how much you value the relationship. To the prospective client who's been sent to you, the gesture illustrates the kind of professionalism you bring to your business every day.

To develop an effective referral reward program, brainstorm ideas with your staff. Aim to create the kind of rewards that you'd appreciate from someone yourself. And then make sure you apply the program consistently.

Work With Mortgage Companies & Realtors

For years, statistics have consistently shown that people tend to move their place of residence several times in their life, even if that move is only across town. Given the rapid pace in which we live, that's not likely to change, and that's good news for you because people on the move are terrific sources for potential new business. While they're setting up house-keeping and scoping out the neighborhood for good wallpaper shops, they may well be in the market for insurance, too. Obviously, you don't have time to pursue them door to door, but that doesn't mean you can't target them another way.

Indeed, one solid strategy for bringing them into your loop is by making buddies with the mortgage companies and realtors in your area. They have a vested interest in knowing who's moving into town and who's moving out. And they're just as grateful for professional associations as you are. By staying in touch with mortgage companies and Realtors on a consistent basis you can work toward a cooperative relationship that leads to referrals for you. You may not get to those new neighbors before the wallpaper goes up, but you don't have to be far behind.

Participate In Welcome Newcomers

If you've ever bought a house, you're probably familiar with "Welcome Newcomers" or "Welcome Wagon" programs that target new homeowners with material about businesses in their neighborhood. Your local chamber of commerce can probably tell you if such a program exists in your area, and if it does, leap on it and participate! Provide the "welcome" people with something from your agency to include in the packet of material they pass out. The programs can help you get a foot in the door.

Typically, participation means you provide an incentive for new homeowners to swing by your agency. The incentive is often a gift, like a home safety kit, and even if it isn't expensive, people new to an area tend to be receptive. After all, they're making a lot of decisions and one of those decisions may well involve insurance. There's no reason in the world you shouldn't be there to help them make up their minds.

Build Relationships With Centers of Influence

"Centers of Influence" are people in the community and even in your agency who are interested in seeing you succeed, and seem both able and inclined to direct quality business your way. It may be that they want you to succeed because your business adds a professional touch to the neighborhood. Or perhaps they're interested in your success because of your involvement in their own community programs. For any number of reasons, centers of influence are people who have come to respect and admire you, and they're willing to reach for referrals on your behalf.

Business owners, neighborhood association leaders, people involved in local government, clergy . . . any of them may be in positions to help you do well–and for that matter, you may well be a "center of influence" for them, too.

Your relationships with these people may spring from situations that have little or nothing to do with your business on a day-to-day basis. Or they may be intricately involved. Either way, good relationships can be advantageous all around, and they're worth fostering.

Stay in touch with your centers of influence on a regular basis. Keep them involved, and include them in your referral reward program. Let them know they're a real part of your team–because they are!

....

Troy's Bottom Line: It's not one big thing that makes marketing successful. It's a combination of all the little things done consistently that brings new clients to your door–and keeps existing clients from going elsewhere.

....

SIMPLIFY AND SEE SALES SWELL!

We all remember at least one despairing time in our careers when the most we could muster toward a sale was one appointment in a day or maybe just one for the entire week. Think back. Your presentation might have gone something like this: "Hey mister, if you don't buy this policy from me I'm going to starve!" All right. Maybe your presentation wasn't that bad, but mine was. Worse, I knew it was bad! But that's what desperation and a lousy strategy will do to a person.

I'm happy to report that I'm past the desperation stage of my career, and you probably are as well. But I wouldn't be surprised if you told me that even though the words come more smoothly now, an effective strategy doesn't. The fact is, it's way too easy to hang sales on a single strategy, and it's downright compelling to make that strategy price. It won't work.

Trying to sell on price isn't a strategy at all. It only masquerades as a strategy, and I guarantee that it'll never bring you to your long-term goals. There will always be a "Shifting Sands Mutual Insurance Company" that can underprice you and take away your business. Oh, sure. You can drop your price even lower, but good old Shifting Sands will be right back at you, and before you know it you're caught up in a vicious circle that no one wins.

The only way out is to shift gears on Shifting Sands by selling on the merits of your product. That requires two things, and both are important.

The first is establishing a philosophy that addresses why people would want to buy your product and your service to begin with. The second is more straightforward—numbers! Whether it's auto, fire, life, commercial, or health insurance you're selling, and whether it's a $500 premium or a $500,000 premium, if you don't get in front of enough people, you'll never hit your stride.

Get the philosophy and get enough people in front of you, and selling becomes painless. It becomes a job of telling your story—simply.

Philosophy and Convictions Do Matter!

I seriously doubt you went into the insurance business because you wanted money for a flashy car and a good set of golf clubs. There are faster ways to make a buck. What I don't doubt is that you went into the business because you believe in its underlying value. You have conviction in it.

Does that sound too "golly-gee-whiz" for the insurance industry? I hope not, because conviction is a big part of the equation for success. Wrap it around the way you do business, and you'll prosper. Try to prosper without conviction and you'll do a fast fade.

So how do you articulate your convictions? How do you translate them into a philosophy that you can bring to every client who sits in your chair?

Start by asking yourself some questions. As you develop your answers, you'll be on your way to a thoughtful mission statement that can guide your business in a way that's consistent with who you are and what you believe in.

You may remember from an earlier chapter that my own father died when I was young, and without insurance my mother simply wouldn't have been able to raise my siblings and me. Obviously, I grew up believing in the value of insurance. But when I reached adulthood and decided to go into the business of selling insurance, I still had to articulate that belief into something concrete, and the only way I could do that was to ask myself some fundamental questions. One was, quite simply, "Why should someone buy insurance from me?"

Answers weren't necessarily automatic. In fact, the very simplicity of the question really forced me to evaluate what I could do. But in the process, something important evolved—my mission statement. It embraces my philosophy in simple terms:

Mission Statement

We are a Farmers Insurance Agency providing
multi-line insurance products to businesses, families,
and individuals in Tulare County and the State of California.
The agency has eleven employees who strive to give
all policyholders the type of service they desire
and have every right to expect.
We take pride in the quality of our products
and the quality of the service we offer.
We bring security and value to those who do business with our Agency.

My mission statement doesn't contain a lot of words, but it does contain my convictions—and a commitment to back them up. By making that mission statement available for the world to see, I'm vowing to help clients make choices that provide appropriate insurance and service. If they get into a car accident and everyone is hurt, I'll be there for them. I'll be there at midnight if their home burns down, and when it comes time to rebuild their home, I'll be there, too.

I'm convinced that having a philosophy that embraces my convictions is what enables me to sell most of my appointments. If you're an agent who's been around for awhile, remind yourself what you're doing for people, and clearly articulate your own philosophy. If you're a new agent, talk to someone who's been in the business, and become convinced about what you do. As you gain experience, build those convictions and formulate a philosophy to guide your business. You won't regret it.

Succeed With the Numbers Game

Insurance is a numbers game, but you don't need to pull out a calculator to do the math on the numbers that matter the most: You need to get to in front of eight to ten people a day if you're looking to grow your agency. And the people you're aiming for are those who believe in insurance and who buy for personal service. Your time is too valuable to try and make a believer out of anyone.

Remember, though, you don't have to go it alone. A dedicated Agency Contact Representative is the magic bullet who can bring in the prequalified leads you need, and that's ninety percent of the sell! The remaining ten percent is up to you, but if you have great products and service, there's no reason in the world to think you won't get the rest of the business, too—*if* you want it. Sometimes, you might not.

Turn Away Price Shoppers

You're not operating a grocery store. You're operating an insurance agency and your products don't go on sale with screaming red stickers. But you will run into people whose only concern is price. They're the ones who will happily troll for "the best price" through the Internet, the Yellow Pages and TV. For them, coverage is secondary.

You know them. You've heard them: "How much is it going to cost? What's the bottom line? Can you give me a quote over the phone?"

Well, if your instincts are to blurt out prices in the interest of capturing a fast sale, you risk being blown way off the course you set when you originally set out your goals. You also risk compromising the philosophy that governs what you believe in.

Look, if I give quotes to potential clients over the phone, the likelihood that they're watching television while I'm trying to explain coverage is pretty high. That means I simply can't do justice to meeting their insurance needs, and those kinds of potential clients aren't for me. They don't jibe with the convictions I have about the value of what I'm selling. Really, they're looking for that "Shifting Sands Mutual Insurance Company," and that's where I refer them.

Are you beginning to understand how what we do is really a numbers game? Directing someone to the nearest Shifting Sands would be really tough if a price shopper was your first appointment of the week and it's already Friday. But if you talk to ten people a day, and twenty percent of them are just interested in price, you can afford to turn them away. You still have a lot of people to see who will buy what you have to offer. You might even be inclined to give the price shoppers bus fare to Shifting Sands.

Mind you, there are occasions when people might sound like price shoppers, but they really aren't. You have to learn how to "read" what they're actually saying. You have to ferret out what their real objectives are. Price may indeed be one of them—perhaps even a significant one—but don't overlook the possibility that it's not the total equation.

Techniques for making those kinds of distinctions could fill another whole book and don't belong in this one. However, I will say that if you commit to reading enough material or listening to enough tapes about communication and listening, you can learn how to accurately assess what's really at stake. I've done that, and I've also talked to lots of sales people who have shared their insights. By now, I know price shoppers when I see them coming, and I gently turn them away. The others I welcome–and sell them.

Just Say No to Unqualified Customers

Sometimes, it's hard to say "no" when you should. In fact, the biggest trouble I've ever managed to walk myself into has occurred when I tried to help someone with a questionable risk or situation I really couldn't accept. It's an easy mistake to make, especially if trying to help is a part of who you are.

Resist. You'll waste your time, and you might forfeit your image with the client because when you ultimately do have to confess that you can't help, the client will think you're unprofessional. Ouch.

Your best bet–tough as it is–is to let unqualified clients know up front that for whatever reasons, they don't fit into what you do. That's all right. You don't just operate some garden-variety agency and, because you don't, not everybody can fit. Simply learn to say, "I'm sorry, I can't help you." The time you spend worrying about people you have to turn away is far better spent working with the people you *can* help.

Learning to say no won't hurt your business, either. Think about the math again. Your goal is to get yourself in front of eight to ten people a day. Turn away one or two here and there and you're still seeing plenty of people who are qualified and interested in more than price. That's the cream of the crop. You don't have to hard sell them. You just have to tell your story.

Tell Your Story - Simply

I remember my very first attempt to sell insurance. My mind was going in a thousand directions, but as I drove out to the appointment, I recalled a key piece of advice from my manager, "Look, Troy," he said, "if you just tell your story the best you can and you're honest, clients will feel sorry for you and help you out."

I got to my destination and started explaining how our auto policy worked. During my explanation on liability, things went well. Real well. But when I got to the portion about uninsured motorists, it was another story altogether, because I hadn't had the class on uninsured motorist. I couldn't answer questions because I didn't know the answers myself. Let's talk *embarrassment*!

I wound up getting on the phone to call my manager at home. I said, "I'm out on an appointment and I know you're eating dinner, but the lady wants to know what uninsured motorist is all about. I don't know what to tell her."

He said, "Troy, tell her that fifty-one percent of the people in our area don't carry insurance, so she needs coverage for uninsured motorist." I turned around and said, "He says you need that." I think the woman felt so sorry for me that she literally helped me fill out the application.

I always chuckle when I think back to that appointment. But the one thing I gained from that night, besides a commission, was a valuable lesson: Tell your story, and tell it with conviction, and people will buy!

What I've learned since is to also tell my story simply. Put another way, this time by French moralist Luc, Marquis De Vauvenargues:

"When a thought is too weak to be expressed simply, it should be rejected."

The Marquis will get no argument from me! Insurance, even life insurance, is simple and easy to understand if it's presented in simple terms. Where things fall apart is when we assume the poor guy across the desk has the desire and ability to absorb in thirty minutes what took most of us weeks to learn. When we let that happen, all we do is confuse our client, and confused clients don't buy insurance.

Of course, many agents have effective presentations and I'm not suggesting you replace yours with mine. But if you're trying to shore up your approach or want specifics on how to tell your story simply, here's a four-step process that works for me in thirty minutes or less:

The Short Course on Who I Am

First, I don't assume my clients necessarily know much about my company or agency, so I take a few minutes to tell them. After all, I want them to understand they're dealing with a professional, and one who genuinely cares. In that context, I also take advantage of the opportunity to brag a little and remind them of why they came to me. My goal is to make sure they understand that my agency is unique. Some of the discussion material I use comes from the Agency History and Agency Overview that you'll find in Appendix A.

Let's Talk Product

After I've painted a broad picture of my agency, I get right into

the products I sell and service, and I explain to clients what my products

can do for them. Remember, I'm only going after clients who I already

know are interested in insurance, so I don't have to waste time talking

about the importance of it. I can safely assume that if they've taken the

time to come to an appointment in my office, they're interested.

At this point, it might seem logical to whip out a chart or comput-

er-generated proposal. And in fact, I might indeed have all that information

tucked away in their file for my own use. But my intent is to explain my

product in simple terms, not to waylay them with complex figures that

won't do anything but cloud the issue. There are better ways to go about

explaining details, and I save it for the next step.

Simple Pictures Sell Products Simply

The best gizmo in the world isn't a gizmo at all. It's a nine-buck

white board that uses markers and a dry eraser. Its greatest value is in its low-tech features, which allow me to explain my products in uncomplicated terms. It absolutely turns seeing into believing without giving anyone a headache in the process.

All I have to do to explain the complexities of a product I'm discussing with clients is draw little diagrams on the board. I can scribble squares and circles and stick figures a lot faster than I can describe some fancy graph, and doing that wows clients more than any computer proposal ever could.

For one thing, simple pictures can show complicated material in simple ways–an especially handy approach for getting into the intricacies of life insurance. Clients appreciate that. But they also like that I'm drawing a picture that's specific to their circumstances–and I'm doing it just for them. They know I'm not pulling out a "one size fits all" chart that I've used a thousand times before.

I've given this kind of "white board" presentation to doctors, lawyers and accountants, and everyone in between. A lot of them comment that they never understood how insurance–particularly life insurance–really worked until they saw it go up on my board. It's a small step from that kind of reception to making a sale, and I almost always do. So move over, da Vinci. Competition is everywhere!

The Wrap-Up

When I've said what I have to say, I conclude my presentation with a brief discussion intended to convey my philosophy. It sounds something like this: "I offer something you need, and I want to be the one to help you with it. I'm not always the cheapest and I'm not always the most expensive. I am the one who will always be there and the one you're going to tell your friends about."

It's that simple.

....

Troy's Bottom Line: You're in a numbers game. If you play it right and back your approach to sales with conviction and simplicity, you'll win in a big way—and with honor.

....

A FINAL THOUGHT

Ours is a dynamic business, and it's fiercely competitive. Every day brings new choices and new decisions, and the decisions you make can spell the difference between stagnation and success. But you don't have to be like a moth beating its wings against an outside light. If you set goals that mirror your convictions, and if you follow through with the strategies I've described, most people will buy from you.

And the ones who don't? Let them go and move on. You now know how to keep enough people in front of you to turn this numbers game of ours into an advantage. You have the keys to hold the clients you get. And you have an assortment of tools for building on them. You will succeed.

That moth . . . feel sorry for it if you must, but don't look back.

—Troy Korsgaden

ABOUT THE AUTHOR

Troy Korsgaden is an award-winning agent whose insightful strategies and enthusiasm have made him a popular speaker and motivator at seminars across the United States.

He was named "Agent of the Year" for the Farmers Insurance Group of Companies in 1995 and again in 1997 after distinguishing himself from a pool of more than 14,000 candidates. He has received numerous other awards as well, including the Personal Lines Agent of the Year for 1993/94 and Preferred Underwriting Agent for eight consecutive years.

Mr. Korsgaden, who launched his own agency in 1983, doubled his agency size in just three years and annually averages a net gain in policies of 750. He has shared his formula for success with small and large agencies alike, and conducts as many as twelve seminars monthly.

Mr. Korsgaden, the "agent's agent," resides in Visalia, California with his wife, Catherine, and two children, Michael and Emily.

APPENDIX A
MARKETING PLAN EXAMPLE

TROY KORSGADEN INSURANCE
1998 MARKETING PLAN
January 1, 1998 - December 31, 1998

Troy Lee Korsgaden
Central Park Professional Center
1700 West Walnut Avenue, Suite A
Visalia, CA 93277
(559) 625-4926
(559) 625-1603 fax

MISSION STATEMENT

We are a Farmers Insurance Agency
providing multi-line insurance products to businesses,
families and individuals in Tulare County
and the State of California.

The Agency has eleven employees
who strive to give all policyholders the type of service
they desire and have every right to expect.

We take pride in the quality of our products
and the quality of the service we offer.

We bring security and value to those who
do business with our agency.

Agency History

The agency was founded in 1983 by Troy L. Korsgaden. Since then it has expanded to a staff of eleven servicing over 6,350 accounts. The client base consists primarily of the local agricultural industry, small businesses and family-oriented services. The agency offers all lines of insurance, specializing in auto, homeowners, life, commercial and health. The agency takes pride in its high sales volume, all-lines profitability, balanced production and technical competence. Its biggest competitors are State Farm in personal lines and Buckman Mitchell, Inc., in commercial. Troy Korsgaden is a member of the Farmers Insurance Presidents Council, which consists of less than 1 percent of the entire agency force in the U.S. In addition, Troy has received the following honors:

- Farmers Insurance Group All-Lines Agent of the Year – 1996/1997
  (From among 14,000 agents across the United States)
- Farmers Insurance Group Personal Lines Agent of the Year – 1993/1994
  (From among 14,000 agents across the United States)
- Farmers Insurance Group All-Lines Agent of the Year – 1994/1995
  (From among 14,000 agents across the United States)
- Life Champion, Topper's Club, PUA (Preferred Underwriter)
- LUTCF (Life Underwriting Training Council Fellow)
- MDRT Qualifier (Industry Award)

Five-Year Plan

Goal: January 1, 1997 - December 31, 2002

PIF: 9,000   Net Policies in Force
              300   Policies Per Quarter Net Gain
              100   Per Month Net Gain

INCOME: Maintain staff income at 20% above industry level.

STAFFING: Establish fully staffed telemarketing department.
              Hire additional CSRs for each department.

One-Year Plan

Goal: January 1, 1998 - December 31, 1998

PIF: 7,000+   Net Policies in Force
              300   Policies Per Quarter Net Gain
              100   Per Month Net Gain

SELL: 160   Per Month
              40   Per Week

INCOME: 20% Surplus in Payroll Account
              20% Surplus in Operation Account

STAFFING: Licensing of Entire Staff

Auto Marketing Plan

GOALS
- Average 240 Auto count each month
- Keep retention level above 96%

PURPOSE
To support the agency by maintaining a profit in underwriting and to secure cross leads for other departments.

FACT
Auto is the biggest income base for our agency at this time.

STRATEGY
- Use Central Marketing Program
- Use current client x-dates to secure appointments
- Use computer to clean plate in household

STAFFING
- Four Account Executives/Offense-appt.s and calls
- Agency Contact Representative/CSRs-Pivot to cross sell

IMPLEMENTATION
- 200 Count Average - April 1, 1998
- Obtain x-dates from each Account Executive
- Average 2 appointments per day for each Account Executive

Fire Marketing Plan

GOALS
- Average 300 Fire count each month
- Maintain profit in underwriting
- Keep retention level above 96%

PURPOSE
To maintain fire growth and expand referral sources from Realtors and Title offices.

FACT
Our agency has grown in the past through fire marketing. There are many cross sale potentials in this area.

STRATEGY
- Use Central Marketing Program
- Expand referral sources by using one day each week to call on Realtors
- Fully utilize Computer/Comments/X-Dating Program

STAFFING
- Four Account Executives
- Agency Contact Representative/CSR- Pivot to cross sell

IMPLEMENTATION
- 300 Count Average - Feb, 1998

Life Marketing Plan

GOALS
- Average 20 new policies each month
- Keep Life Lapse Ratio below 5.0%
- Average 1670 life count each month

PURPOSE
To increase commission to agency for future growth as well as increase bonus income for agency profit.

FACT
Life commissions and bonuses have funded all past agency growth.

STRATEGY
- Four leads from each Account Executive every day
- Life sales through policy reviews
- Use Central Marketing Program
- VIP - CPA & Attorney Leads program
- Mortgage Insurance Program

STAFFING
- Four Account Executives
- Agency Contact Representatives/CSRs

IMPLEMENTATION
- 20 Life Policies - Feb., 1998
- Implement VIP Program by April, 1998

Commercial Marketing Plan

GOALS
- Average 10 applications each month
- Average 300 count each month
- Maintain profit in underwriting
- $700,000 in new business premium for year

PURPOSE
To increase commission and increase underwriting bonus potential for agency. To secure additional cross selling leads.

FACT
This will be our agency's biggest premium growth area.

STRATEGY
- Central Marketing Program
- Target Marketing X-Dates
- Referral Program
- Computerized Servicing & Solicitation

STAFFING
- Comm'l Sales Manager
- Office Director
- Four Account Executives
- Agency Contact Representative

IMPLEMENTATION
- 300 Count Average - March 1998

Health Marketing Plan

GOALS
- $700,000 in new health premium

PURPOSE
To provide all lines service, increase agency commission base and open doors to new commercial accounts.

FACT
Health is a need for clients that is not being serviced by other all-lines agencies.

STRATEGY
- Commercial and Personal leads to be called on and followed up in the same manner as our P&C business
- Use Central Marketing Program

STAFFING
- Agency Contact Representative
- Four Account Executives
- CSR

IMPLEMENTATION
- Well organized health operation using our current computer and office follow-up
- Central Marketing by January 2, 1998

Claims Service Plan

GOALS
- Rapid reporting of all losses to facilitate rapid settlement
- Consistent return of phone calls in a timely manner
- Get our "B" parties to change companies to us

PURPOSE

To live up to the promise that we will be active in each claim.
To give each client the best settlement for their claim dollar.

FACT

Claims are the only true service we can give our clients.

STRATEGY
- Cross-train all producers to key in losses in the event the claims person is out of the office
- Maintain positive relationships with all claims staff, rental car companies, body shops, etc...

STAFFING
- Agency Claims Representative/Agency Support Implementation
- Cross train as needed for filling out L.R.'s, and keying in of, claims

Marketing Operations Plan

GOALS
- To increase each line of insurance in this agency by no less than 30%

PURPOSE
To have multiple lines of insurance in every household increasing the bottom line and retention making the agency, "The place to have all your insurance."

FACT
In every department we need to plant seeds and pass referrals to other departments.

STRATEGY
- Use four policy review appointments
- Inform clients of one stop agency: commercial, health, etc. and establish next target market
- Utilize staff meetings for cross account marketing
- On-going training for Agency Contact Representatives
- Central Marketing

STAFFING
- Account Executive
- CSR
- Agency Contact Representative

IMPLEMENTATION
- Add marketing update to staff meeting agenda by March, 1998

Financial Plans

GOALS
- To establish a six month operating expense reserve

PURPOSE
To have financial stability for growth and business catastrophic change.

FACT
Payroll and income needs must be stated at beginning of each year. Sales goals set to meet need.

STRATEGY
- Develop operating budget, specifying operating and marketing expenses for each department
- Generate monthly statement of operations listing department expenditures and sales production

STAFFING
- Accounts Payable Manager
- Office Director

IMPLEMENTATION
- Establish budget by April 1, 1998
- Establish sales and expense report by June 1, 1998

APPENDIX B
FORMS

Forms Content

Following are a number of forms you may find useful in applying approaches discussed in Power Position Your Agency; A Guide to Insurance Agency Success!

Form Title	Purpose
Household Update Sheet	Gather uniform information for client files.
Hot List	Identify and track individuals with high potential for sales and/or referrals.
Five Focus Goals	Keep priority goals top of mind for short- to medium-term action.
Employee Prospect	Identify and track individuals with high potential for employment.
Auto Proposal Sheet	Provide information for an auto proposal.
Vesting/Fire Proposal Sheet	Provide information for a fire proposal.
Life Solicitation Form	Provide underwriting information for a life proposal.
Life Prospect Form	Track potential life customers.
Life Checklist	Ensure we issue the life case opened.
Auto Claims Form	Ensure we handle auto claims consistently.
Property Claims Form	Ensure we handle property claims consistently.
Call Follow-Up Tool	Ensure that calls are followed up and/or returned.
Agency Marketing Survey	Create a conversation that provides x-dates and referrals.
Commercial Dept. Checklist	Provide consistent and detailed information for commercial sales.

Auto Proposal Sheet

Name:_____ Date:_____

Address:_____

Referred by:_____ Appointment Y N Date:_____

Phone: (Wk)_____ (Hm)_____

Residence Type:

Private dwelling   Apartment   Condo/Townhouse   Mobile Home: owned   rented

Farm   Military   Other:_____

Quote also: FIRE   LIFE   HEALTH   COMMERCIAL

Driver Information	Vehicle #1	Vehicle #2	Vehicle #3
Vehicle: Yr/Make/Model			
Date Lic. received			
SSN			
GPA (if GS appl)			
Citation/5 yrs			
Accident/ 5 yrs			
Current Mileage			
Current Carrier			
Current Premium			
Current Liability limits			
Current Deductibles			
Lienholder Info			
VIN			
Quote as: Full/Lia			

Payment Method Preferred: Monthly / Standard

Producer:_____

Vesting/Fire Proposal Sheet

Name: _____ DOB:_____ SSN:_____

Name: _____ DOB:_____ SSN:_____

Address:_____

Phone: (Wk)_____ (Hm)_____

Age of oldest insured: _____ Smokers: Y/N How long in area: _____

Occupation: _____ Years: _____

Any Losses in last 3 years: _____

DWELLING INFORMATION

Number of Units: 1) single   2) duplex   3) triplex   4) fourplex   DP1 _____

Style: 1 story   1-1/2 stories   2 stories   bi-level   split level   TH   DP2 _____

Year of Construction: _____ Total square feet: _____ DP3 _____

Basement: Y/N   Garage#cars: _____   Attached/Detached/Built-In

Alarm system: _____ Local: _____ Central Servicing Company: _____ Prior Insurance Y/N

Roof type: _____ Age of Roof: _____ How long at residence: _____

Exterior walls (enter as a %)

___ wood siding   ___ alum/vinyl siding   ___ brick veneer

___ stone veneer   ___ stucco on frame   ___ solid brick

___ solid stone   ___ asbestos shingles   ___ wood shake

___ paint on masonry   ___ stucco on masonry   ___ adobe

Heating/Cooling: _____ Heat only _____ Heat and A/C

Interior Walls: _____ Drywall/Sheetrock _____ Plaster Baths(enter #): _____

Fireplaces: _____ Insert or Woodburing Stove: _____

Other (check all that apply):

___ Open Porch/Breezeway   ___ Screened Porch/Breezeway   ___ Deck

___ Solar Panels   ___ Skylights   ___ Exterior Shutters

Escrow Officer: _____ Phone: _____

Title Company: _____ Fax#: _____ Prematic# _____

Loan Number _____ Impound Acct: Y/N Loan Amount _____ Sales Price _____

Flood Ins. Required: Y/N   Elevation Certificate: Y/N

Current Carrier: _____ Policy Number: _____

Realtor: _____ Phone: _____

Life Solicitation

Name _____

Address _____

City/State/Zip _____

Home Phone _____ Work Phone _____

Name	DOB	Smoker

Life Prospect

Name _____

Address _____

City/State/Zip _____

Home Phone _____ Work Phone _____

1st Call _____

2nd Call _____

3rd Call _____

4th Call _____

5th Call _____

6th Call _____

Appointment _____

Sold _____

Follow-up _____

Life Checklist

Name _____

Address _____

City/State/Zip _____

Home Phone _____ Work Phone _____

Policy # _____ Underwriter _____

[ ] Approach _____

[ ] Appointment 1 _____

[ ] Appointment 2 _____

[ ] Application _____

[ ] Thank You Letter _____

[ ] Medical Ordered _____

[ ] Medical Completed _____

[ ] Additional Requirements _____

[ ] Referral Letter Requested _____

[ ] Delivery _____

[ ] 4 Month Follow-Up Call _____

[ ] Hold File for 1 Year Annual Life Review & Retirement Review _____

Property Claims Form

Date Reported_____ Type of Claim_____ Subrogation: Y   N

Date of Loss_____ Claim #_____ Policy # _____

Adjuster _____ Deductible _____

Insured _____ Hm# _____ Wk#_____

Insurance Information/Notes Regarding Loss

_____
_____
_____
_____
_____
_____
_____
_____
_____
_____
_____

Claim History

Date	Initials	Time	Remarks

Call Follow-Up Tool

Policy #	Name	Problem	Solution	Phone

Commercial Department Checklist

DBA _____

Name _____

Address _____

City/State/Zip _____

Phone _____ Fax _____

Contact _____ Title _____

Type of Business _____

Appointment _____

X-Dates

Liability _____ Health _____

W/C _____ Disability _____

Auto _____ Umbrella _____

Fire _____ Life _____

Notes

_____
_____
_____
_____
_____
_____

Proposal Typed _____

Presentation Appointment _____

Hot List

Date	Name	Phone	Appt. Set	Comments

Employee Prospect

Name _____

Address _____

City/State/Zip _____

Home Phone _____
Work Phone _____
Mobile Phone _____
Pager _____

Current Employer _____

Current Position / Title _____

Where would this person fit in our office?

_____
_____
_____
_____
_____

Five Focus Goals

Goal #1 _____

_____

Action Plan:

A_____

B_____

C_____

D_____

Goal #2 _____

_____

Action Plan:

A_____

B_____

C_____

D_____

Goal #3 _____

_____

Action Plan:

A_____

B_____

C_____

D_____

Goal #4 _____

_____

Action Plan:

A_____

B_____

C_____

D_____

Goal #5 _____

_____

Action Plan:

A_____

B_____

C_____

D_____

Auto Claims Form

Date Reported _____ Type of Claim _____ Subrogation: Yes / No

Date of Loss _____ Claim # _____ Policy # _____

Adjuster PD _____ Adjuster BI _____

Insured _____

Home Phone _____ Work Phone _____

Driver _____

Home Phone _____ Work Phone _____

SR1- Date Form Sent _____ Deductible _____

Body Shop / Vehicle Location _____

Car Rental Coverage: Yes / No   Type _____

Claimant Insurance Information / Notes Regarding Loss

_____
_____
_____
_____

Claim History

Date	Initials	Time	Remarks

Agency Marketing Survey

Name _____

Address _____

City/State/Zip _____

Home Phone _____ Work Phone _____

1. Why did you buy through our agency?

_____
_____

2. Do you carry other types of insurance? When do these policies renew?

Auto _____

Home _____

Life _____

Commercial _____

Health _____

Recreational Vehicle _____

CDs and T-Bills _____

3. Do you have any other questions about your present insurance program?

_____
_____

4. Do you have a friend or relative that may be unhappy with their insurance or be in situation similar to yours?

[No] We would appreciate your giving a friend or relative our name and numbers.

[Yes] May we have their name and number?

_____
_____

Household Update Sheet

Name _____ _____

Address _____

City/State/Zip _____

Home Phone _____ Fax _____

Mr. Work _____ Mrs. Work _____

Mr. Fax _____ Mrs. Fax _____

Mr. Cell _____ Mrs. Cell _____

Mr. Pager _____ Mrs. Pager _____

	Currently Insured With	Expiration Date
Auto		
Home		
Rental		
Life		
Comm'l		
Umbrella		
Rec. Vehicle		
Retirement		
Health		

Emergency Contact

Name _____
Address _____
City / State / Zip _____
Home Phone _____ Work Phone _____

APPENDIX C
AGENCY CONTACT
REPRESENTATIVE SCRIPTS

X-Date Script

Hello Mr./Mrs. _____. This is_____ calling from Troy Korsgaden Insurance Agency.

How are you this morning/evening? Is this a good time to talk?

Mr./Mrs. _____, the reason I'm calling is that our company is very competitive in the home/auto/commercial insurance market, and we were wondering if you would be interested in a competitive quote for your home/auto the next time it comes up for renewal.

When does your insurance come up for renewal?

Mr./Mrs. _____, we will give you a call 60-90 days before the renewal and put together a quote to see if you're getting the best value for your insurance dollar.

Thank you once again, Mr./Mrs. _____.

X-Date Follow-Up Script

Hello Mr./Mrs. _____. This is _____ calling from Troy
Korsgaden Insurance Agency.

How are you? Is this a good time to talk?

The reason I'm calling is that our office had given you a call a while back
regarding your auto/home/commercial insurance, and you said it would be
coming up for renewal around this time and that you may be interested in
getting a competitive quote to see if you're getting the best buy for your
insurance dollar.

Mr./Mrs. _____, at this time I would like to get a little information
from you regarding your auto/home/commercial in order to put together a
competitive quote for you.

(Using form, take information.)

Mr./Mrs. _____, Troy realizes that you're extremely busy. What we
would like to do is schedule an appointment to come into our office whenever it is most convenient for you, so that Troy can go over this valuable
information. It should take no more than 15-20 minutes.

What would you prefer, mornings or afternoons?

(Set the appointment.)

Remember:
   • *The appointment will last less than half an hour (15-20 minutes)*

Life and Retirement Script

Hello Mr./Mrs. _____. this is _____ calling from Troy Korsgaden Insurance Agency.

Is this a good time to talk?

Mr./Mrs. _____, we are pleased that we have been able to serve you with your personal insurance needs.

The reason I'm calling is that Troy was reviewing your file and he noticed that we do not carry your life / retirement insurance. Do you have those at work? How much? What policies do you own outside of work?

In the event of a tragedy, Mr./Mrs. _____, and I'm not trying to frighten you today because the odds are it will never happen, but if there were a tragedy and our office was called, Troy needs this very valuable information to assist your family members by having information on who to call and how much you have. This is very valuable, right, Mr./Mrs. _____?

What we would like to do is set aside some personal time for you to meet with Troy to update your confidential file and review your current program.

We will work around your schedule. What would be the best time to set up a personal meeting with Troy? Do you prefer mornings or afternoons?

(Set the appointment.)

Remember:
- *The appointment will last less than half an hour (15-20 minutes)*
- *This initial appointment is to review current life/ retirement policies and identify needs—it is not a sales appointment*

Review Appointment

Hello, is this Mr./Mrs. _____? This is _____ from Troy Korsgaden's Insurance Agency.

How are you this morning/afternoon? Is this a good time to talk?

Mr./Mrs. _____, we are pleased that we have been able to serve you with your insurance needs.

And the reason I'm calling today is Troy would like to set aside some time to get together with you and review the coverage that you have with our office. We want to make sure that your coverage is up-to-date and adequate, and make sure that you're getting every discount that may be available to you. And we can do all this in a 15-20 minute appointment with Troy.

Mr./Mrs. _____, Troy informed me that you are very busy, and I'll do my best to work around your schedule. Which is usually the best time for you? Do you prefer mornings or afternoons?

(Set the appointment.)

Remember:
> • *The appointment will last less than half an hour
> (15-20 minutes)*

APPENDIX D
JOB DESCRIPTIONS

CSR–Customer Service Representative
(Auto, Fire, Life, Commercial, Health)

- Process applications
- Process coverage charges
- Assist insured with billing and coverage inquiries
- Track and verify completion of all policy activities
- Take the opportunity to transition for additional coverage during daily contact with insured
- Obtain necessary information from insured and prepare proposals

Account Executive
(Auto, Fire, Life, Commercial, Health)

- Meet with and present quotations to insured
- Review and advise insured on policy coverage needs for existing business as well as additional coverage needs
- Solicit new business/seek referrals

Receptionist

- Answer all calls in a timely manner
- Greet clients
- Process premium payments
- Update insured's information (such as phone numbers) whenever possible
- Assist with agency mailings
- Print daily calendars and secure client folders previously prepared for all appointments
- Assist clients whenever possible with billing questions

Agency Claims Representative

- Input all loss reports taken
- Work with insured to assist with immediate needs at time of loss
- Keep detailed documentation of all contact with insured, claims office, other party, etc.
- Follow up with insured upon completion of loss to ensure satisfaction
- Special office projects assigned as time allows

Agency Contact Representative

- Schedule 4 review appointments, 2 P&C, 2 Life, and 2 Commercial appointments
- Schedule appointment or obtain x-date information from marketing sources
- Maintain appointment calendars
- Create marketing plans with agent
- Create and obtain lists
- Coordinate external marketing

Office Manager

- Act as executive assistant to agent (Troy)
- Follow up and direct necessary information to appropriate department to complete promise to insured as result of appointment with agent
- Maintain personnel files: payroll, vacation/sick leave, quarterly reviews, etc.
- Track production and servicing of each department
- Update employees via quarterly interoffice newsletter of important marketing, customer service and underwriting issues

Accounts Payable

- Upkeep Premium account
- Maintain trust account
- Make daily bank deposit
- Process agency account payables
- Oversee Budget

An executive workshop to develop a strategic
and tactical plan for agency growth.

Unleash the Power of your Agency.

TROY'S 1-DAY EXECUTIVE WORKSHOP

Troy Korsgaden has put into action his vision for the ultimate agency—a multi-line agency that delivers a broad array of products with a focus on delivering the type of service his clients deserve and have every right to expect. Troy shares his knowledge, experience and innovative systems in this one-day executive workshop in which **you will learn how to:**

- **Develop your vision for the future**

- **Balance your book of business for maximum profits**

- **Build a high performance team, each person as a profit center**

- **Jumpstart sales while increasing client retention**

- **Use innovative marketing techniques delivering sustainable results**

VISIT US ONLINE FOR CURRENT DATES AND A LOCATION NEAR YOU.

www.tksystems.org
(800) 524-6390

TROY
KORSGADEN
SYSTEMS

TKSystems, 1700 West Walnut Avenue, Suite A, Visalia, CA 93277